GOLFERS GIVING BACK

Exceptional Charity Tournaments
Coast to Coast

Joel Zuckerman

Library of Congress Catalog Number: 2015946679

ISBN: 9781513602257

Published by Saron Press, Ltd., Ridgeland, South Carolina 29936
www. saronpress.com
Email: info@saronpress.com

First Edition

Printed in Hong Kong

Books may be purchased in quantity and/or special sales
by contacting the author at: www.vagabondgolfer.com
Email: info@vagabondgolfer.com

Thoughts on Charity...
and

Charity Golf Events

I don't know of any other organization that's raised more money than golf has, because if you are a baseball player, you're a football player, you're a hockey player, if you're just a businessman, and you want to raise some money for a charity, what do they do? They have a golf tournament. They have a golf outing, and they go out and they do it.

- Lee Trevino

Almost every Monday I have a charity thing. I like that. I do.

- Yogi Berra

Did universal charity prevail, earth would be a heaven, and hell a fable.

- Charles Caleb Colton

There are three things being a celebrity is good for: Raising money for charity, dinner reservations and tee times.

- Dennis Quaid

Before prayer, give to charity.

- Nachman of Bratslav

To ease another's heartache is to forget one's own.

- Abraham Lincoln

Acknowledgments

I am indebted to numerous friends, golf professionals, professional golfers, writing colleagues, golf buddies and new acquaintances who made spot-on suggestions for charity golf events that deserved inclusion in this book, or were otherwise helpful in making this ambitious project a reality.

These thoughtful people include:

Jan Albert, Brian Armstrong, Tom Bedell, Larry Biester, Ken Carter, Rick Castillo, Donovan Childers, Rob Clements, A.G. Crockett, Beth Daniel, Paul deVere, Billy Dillon, Jim Dills, Randy Dodson, Eric Eshleman, Sam Eskew, Tom Fitzgerald, Bob Ford, Claude Franco, Kevin Frisch, Dan Gerstman, Michael Gibson, Kevin Hammer, Laurie Hammer, Adam Hemeon, Kay Higby, Stephen Jakab, Gretchen Johnson, David Kass, Brad King, Charlie King, Paul Kruger, Janet Leach, Scott Lincicome, Cindy Mardenfeld, Michael Marion, Kevin Meredith, Pete Michalowski, Michael Moore, Emmy Moore Minister, Ron Montesano, Eric Nadelman, Franklin Newell, Gregg Novick, Teddie O'Keefe, John Patterson, Mac Plumart, Micki Purcell, Michael Reinsch, Jeff Renzulli, Bill Replogle, Tim Riviere, Dave Robinson, Dave Rafus, Jeremy Rudock, John Rusbosin, Dave Ryan, Bill Safrin, Loren Shapiro, Jeff Shelley, Dan Shepherd, Christian Sherbert, Jack Sibbach, Brian Sleeman, Garrett Smithson, Shel Solow, Mary C. Spain, John Steinbreder, Dave Stockton, Mitchell Stump, Jim Sykes, Mike Trenham, Pete Trenham, Justin Tupper, Deb Waitkus, Walt Wandell, Mike Whitaker, Ken Woods, Brad Worthington, Jeff Yost, Mike Zaranek, Karli Zuckerman and Rudy Zupetz.

Thank you for all your help – I am greatly appreciative.

Dedication

This book is dedicated to Dave Rafus and Dave Stockton

The former anonymous, the latter synonymous with Ryder Cup
success and championship golf.

It was Dave R. who provided me the simple, but heretofore
unexplored book concept. It was Dave S. who rode in like a white
knight as the project meandered mid-stream, and was instrumental
in getting it to the finish line.

Simply put: I wouldn't have begun without the suggestion of Rafus.
I couldn't have finished without the assistance of Stockton.

Thank You, Gentlemen!

Also by

Joel Zuckerman

Golf in the Lowcountry
2003

Golf Charms of Charleston
2005

Misfits on the Links
2006

A Hacker's Humiliations
2007

Pete Dye Golf Courses – Fifty Years of Visionary Design
2008

Kiawah Golf – The Game's Elegant Island
2011

Pro's Pros
2013

About the Author

Veteran golf, travel and sports writer Joel Zuckerman is the author of seven previous books, two of which were honored as Book of the Year by the International Network of Golf at the annual PGA Show in Orlando, Florida.

Zuckerman has contributed features, profiles and essays to more than one hundred different magazines, newspapers and web sites. These include some of the best known sports and airline magazines, and virtually all of the major golf publications.

As a professional speaker, he has entertained at book festivals, corporate events, conventions, tournaments, country clubs and on cruise ships.

He and his wife Elaine live in Utah and Georgia.

For more information visit: vagabondgolfer.com

Table of Contents

Foreword

I turned professional in 1964, and have clear memories of numerous moments in my career.

I know the name of the first pro tournament I entered, my playing partner that day, and what I shot. I can recall tournaments won, some squandered, and others where a competitor played wonderfully to win down the stretch. I am well aware of my playoff record, both on the regular and Champions Tours, but will spare my own ego and avoid specifics.

I have clear memories of the Ryder Cup, as a player, captain and vice-captain. My partners, our opponents, and who came away with the victories.

However I could never hazard a guess as to exactly how many charity golf events I've participated in. It might be north of one thousand. It's not like I was more altruistic than my peers, we all were doing the same thing. Contemporaries like Palmer, Nicklaus, Player, Casper, Trevino, Watson, Irwin, Miller, North and dozens of others were just as involved. The current generation is equally charitable, the biggest difference is that the successful modern players often form their own charitable foundations.

As a longtime member myself, I'm proud to know that the PGA Tour has helped raise over two billion charitable dollars since 1938. But that impressive number is absolutely dwarfed by the staggering amounts of money that have been raised by grassroots charity tournaments like the ones showcased here. The specific amount is uncountable, but nationwide, across the decades, for a thousand or more worthy causes, it is billions upon billions of dollars.

Charity is at the heart of golf, which makes this unique book so relevant. There have been thousands of golf books published in my lifetime, and this is the first one that provides a glimpse into the world of charity golf events.

Author Joel Zuckerman has mined unexplored territory previously. His last book profiled some of the nation's most acclaimed club professionals.

I am friendly with or am acquainted with a number of those profile subjects, and there isn't a more deserving group of individuals in the game. But the book in your hands is even more significant. Instead of writing about an individual, as deserving as they may be, Joel is writing about a cause.

Though only a minute fraction of the charity golf events in the nation are showcased within these pages, the author has done a wonderful job highlighting so many of the varied causes that exist. Children's hospitals, military support groups, environmental issues, battered women's shelters, scholarship funds, memorial events, medical research, grief counseling, literacy awareness, children's homes and golf-specific support groups are just the tip of the iceberg.

Each chapter provides a brief but telling glimpse into the world of that charity golf event. Why it was founded, who was compelled to initiate it, the beneficiaries, and the good it does. The reader will be engaged, informed and inspired by these stories, and their newfound awareness and potential support of these excellent causes can only contribute to the greater good. I'm glad Joel wrote this fine book, and it's my pleasure to write this Foreword.

We've all heard the expression, 'charity begins at home.' As a professional golfer for more than half-a-century, I firmly believe that while it certainly begins at home, charity continues on the golf course.

Dave Stockton
U.S Ryder Cup Captain
Two time Major Champion

Introduction

Look long enough and hard enough, and you'll find a charity basketball tournament to support or participate in. Scour the landscape, and eventually discover a charity softball game. Search high and low, far and wide, and a once-in-a-blue-moon charity darts or bowling event will come across the radar. But for all of these charities, there are a hundred charity golf tournaments, perhaps a thousand. Or more.

Why are the golf events ubiquitous? There are a variety of factors. First, golfers tend to be more affluent and philanthropic than the general populace. Second, it allows the organizers to trumpet the cause and the beneficiaries in a leisurely, measured way. Third, both local and national businesses like to align themselves with and market to the golf crowd, making the procurement of significant tournament sponsorships much easier to accomplish.

Furthermore, there are often personal reasons. Bill and El Sugra of Allentown, Pennsylvania lost their son on 9/11. "It's human nature for the overwhelming majority of people to feel compassion," explains El. "When we lost our son that terrible day, we received that compassion from so many people and it profoundly changed our lives. It seemed natural to help other people. When presented with an idea of a golf tournament to honor our son's name, we seized the opportunity."

Mike Williams is a businessman from Greenville, South Carolina, and has long been involved with a charity event that raises funds for a children's shelter. "The fact is that most businesses have either clients, employees or management that enjoy playing golf, entertaining on a golf course, or using golf as a reward of some sort. Because of the appeal of the game and the event itself, it allows us to fill up the field and let the charity benefit from the proceeds."

The only sporting endeavors with nearly the same presence as golf are the ever-present running and walking events with a charitable bent. Memorial races, Susan G. Komen-sponsored activities, and numerous types of fun runs benefit a wide range of deserving causes. However the big differences are the cost and duration. Running events typically cost fifteen to fifty dollars, and depending on the fitness level of the participant, last from twenty minutes to an hour and a half. Everyone goes home sweaty, satisfied, clutching a race t-shirt and a water bottle. Post-race refreshments are rarely more than sports drinks, bottled water, granola bars and bananas.

By comparison, upscale charity golf events often include a boxed lunch, perhaps a post-round cocktail hour, sit-down dinner, and substantive gifts and prizes. It's a way for the charity to really make an impression on the participants, who spend half, sometimes most of a day learning about the cause, and how they can be supportive. The difference between a running event and golf event in terms of lasting impact on those who choose to participate is like the difference between watching a movie trailer and watching the movie itself.

Golf's downward trend persists unabated. Much to the dismay of the millions who have fallen under its addictive spell, in many ways the game continues to wither—courses are closing, the number of rounds played annually continues to ebb, players are heading to the exits. However there can be no debating the enormous impact that golf continues to make on the charity landscape.

Every year, in every state, there are more charity golf events than can be accurately tallied. The number, hard as it is to believe, approaches 150,000. Twelve million players participate. Billions of dollars are raised for a thousand great causes: military, medical, arts, environmental, religious, educational, assisting the underprivileged, and dozens of other equally noble reasons.

All of these events raise needed funds, promote awareness of important societal problems, and are worthy of exposure. The events showcased in this volume aren't 'better' than thousands of others, nor do they necessarily raise more funds, or provide a greater percentage of gross revenue to the end source. However they are prime examples of golf-centric vehicles used as a tool to assist the wonderful causes supported by millions of benevolent golfers across the map. These events, and ten thousand others that couldn't be showcased, illustrate beautifully the age-old concept of golfers giving back.

Andy North and Friends

Along with three tournaments, Andy North also won hundreds of friends and admirers during his decades-long playing career. So when the two-time U.S. Open champion decided to start raising both the profile of and dollars for the University of Wisconsin Carbone Cancer Center in his hometown of Madison, he didn't have to look far to gather an A-list of attendees. The name of the fundraiser is as straightforward as the cause it benefits: Andy North and Friends.

North's roots in Wisconsin run deep, as he has lived there most of his life. He played his collegiate golf at the University of Florida, but is a rarity among his peers as he eschewed the warm-weather residence relocation that is de rigueur for most tour pros. His support of the center is easy to understand. First off, Dr. Paul Carbone himself treated North's mother for breast cancer decades prior, long before the center was renamed in his honor. As is unfortunately the case with so many families and individuals in the nation, cancer has touched the lives of many in North's orbit. "Both my father and father-in-law died of cancer. I had reconstructive surgery due to skin cancer," he begins, recounting the scourge of scores of professional golfers of his era, before the use of sunscreen became prevalent. "I've also battled prostate cancer."

While North and his wife Susan have been very active in supporting charitable causes around Madison (in particular the Special Olympics) for decades, in 2009 they decided to begin their own event. They wanted to shape something to their own liking, make it very distinctive, and support a deeply felt cause. The Carbone Cancer Center was a natural fit: the right place, right time and right mission.

AND NORTH AND FRIENDS

Benefitting the University of Wisconsin Carbone Cancer Center

Kelly Sitkin is the director of development for the Carbone Cancer Center, and her tenure began just a year or two before the inaugural Andy North and Friends event. "Ours is the only comprehensive cancer center in Wisconsin, and one of only forty or so designated nationwide." Sitkin relates that their special designation by the National Cancer Institute is akin to the Good Housekeeping Seal.

The center specializes in research, patient care, and educating the next generation of physicians. They have about 250 researchers, many of whom are doctors. A research snapshot: Dr. Carbone himself helped develop the drug Tamoxifen, essential in the fight against breast cancer. Their pediatric oncology department is part of the "dream team" as designated by Katie Couric's organization, Stand Up to Cancer, with groundbreaking work being done by Dr. Paul Sondel and colleagues in the field of neuroblastoma.

"At the beginning we weren't sure who would show up, but we wanted to put on something that hadn't been seen before in this area," adds Susan North. She and Andy needn't have worried. The very first year, friends and hall of fame-caliber sportsmen like Tom Watson, baseball's Robin Yount, and Aaron Rodgers of the Green Bay Packers lent their support. They welcomed eighty golfers and nearly three hundred for dinner, raising in excess of $300,000 in year one. Things haven't slowed down since.

"The name of the event is no accident," continues North, for many years known as an expert golf commentator on ESPN. "Susan and I wanted our friends from near and far, well-known and little-known, to come be part of this fundraising effort. We feel fortunate they came initially, and continue to return to Madison annually."

Part of the event's popularity is the wonderful mix of Wisconsinites and those with ties

to the state. In the former category are pro golfers like Jerry Kelly and Steve Stricker, Olympic speed skater and gold medalist Dan Jansen, former UW basketball standout and NBA all-star Michael Finley, the Badgers' current hoops coach Bo Ryan, and former Badger and Olympian Jessie Vetter, considered one of the finest female goalies in ice hockey's history.

The latter category is represented by iconic basketball coach Bobby Knight, baseball hall of famer Paul Molitor, ESPN broadcasters like Scott Van Pelt and Mike Tirico, and major championship-winning golfers like Curtis Strange, Paul Azinger, and Annika Sorenstam.

The competitive aspect of the event is minimized, while the friendliness factor is emphasized. "We try to spread the high-profile attendees around so all the groups get to play a few holes with several of our luminaries," states North.

An offshoot of the golf event is the trivia night, which attracts a younger crowd and not only raises awareness of the Cancer Center, but gets the next generation thinking more seriously about philanthropy. Yet another new event is the annual luncheon, with Wisconsinite and James Beard award winner Tory Miller at the helm.

"Andy's event has been such a wonderful boon for our organization," continues Kelly Sitkin. "It goes beyond the dollars, significant as they are. He is helping get the word out to those around the state that we have this amazing institution right here in Madison, and can help so many of our citizens."

When asked by admiring colleagues at other organizations how to run an event as successfully, Sitkin has a simple, but impossible answer. "I tell them to find figureheads like Andy and Sue North," she relates with a laugh. "They are at every meeting, take part in every conference call, start planning the following year's event within weeks of the one

that just ended, and are fully invested in the entire proceedings. They just want to improve and enhance what we're doing every year."

The auction items available at the pre-tournament dinner are literally priceless. There is dinner with Jack and Barbara Nicklaus on their yacht, preceding a round of golf for the winning foursome at the exclusive Bear's Club in south Florida. There is a behind-the-scenes tour of the Baseball Hall of Fame with member Robin Yount. There is even the chance to play golf with Andy North at the scene of his U.S. Open victories, first Oakland Hills outside of Detroit, then a private jet to Cherry Hills in Denver.

With bucket list bonanzas like these, is it any wonder that more than five million dollars have been raised for the Carbone Cancer Center since 2009? "At first we were just hoping to break even and learn the ropes," concludes Sitkin. "We were thrilled when we netted a nice profit that first year. Looking at where we are now, it's above and beyond everyone's expectations."

Expectations at the center are always high. The money raised by the Andy North and Friends event is earmarked for research. They support high risk, cutting edge research, and in turn, the researchers themselves endeavor to get matching grants from the federal government so they can really sink their teeth into each field of study.

"Other than my family, I think this cause is as important to me as anything else I do," concludes North, taking great satisfaction in doing all he can to help the patients at the Carbone Cancer Center during the most important battle of their lives.

For more information visit: www.andynorthandfriends.com

The Arizona's Children's Charities Celebrity Classic

For more fortunate children, an episode of domestic upheaval might lead to a few nights at Grandma's or bunking in with cousins at a favorite aunt's house. But not all children have that luxury.

In the upstate South Carolina city of Greenville, kids with no other recourse find refuge at Pendleton Place, where they are cared for in a compassionate manner sadly unavailable in their troubled homes where drugs, alcohol, violence, domestic disputes, custody battles and other factors conspire to sap the innocence of childhood. They offer programs that protect, equip and heal vulnerable children, young adults and families. Founded more than forty years ago in 1975, Pendleton Place offers not just a home for abused and neglected youth, but also case management and mentoring services for young adults; supervised visitation, safe custody exchange and parent support groups. In addition they provide family evaluations to identify the root cause of abuse and neglect with recommendations to improve the wellbeing of the child while rebuilding families.

Sadly, business is all too brisk at Pendleton Place and similar facilities nationwide. Statistics show that child abuse is reported every ten seconds and claims the lives of nearly five children daily.

Greenville native Mike Williams owns a manufacturing concern, but years back he also acted as a reserve deputy. In those days he occasionally took children into emergency protective custody, delivering them to Pendleton Place. That led to several

terms on their board, which led to his attendance at their inaugural charity golf event in the late 90's. That round took over six hours to complete, the slog exacerbated by the dwindling reserves of refreshments as the day dragged on. Afterwards he was overheard by the event organizer grumbling to friends, and because of his apparent expertise in running a tournament (he didn't have any) was promptly handed the reins going forward. He hasn't looked back in fifteen years.

"I'll be honest, Pendleton Place is not an easy place to visit," admits the father of four, including teenage triplets. "I was there one time and an eight year-old girl bursts out crying. She didn't understand her homework assignment, and there was nobody around at that moment except me to assist. Wouldn't you know, I head home, and my triplets are doing the exact same homework, but with the fortune of having parents who can help them. The girl at Pendleton Place, through no fault of her own, didn't have the same advantage."

However, the advantages are many to the kind-hearted supporters who play in the Arizona's Children's Classic event each year. The tournament motto is "It's All About the Kids," so in addition to raising vast sums to keep Pendleton Place afloat, the golfers are treated to a first-class day of great food, gifts and live music.

The genesis of the golf event is due to the largesse of two local restaurateurs, Kevin Cox and Mark Craig, original owners of the Arizona's Steak House, which gives the long-standing tournament its name. These socially conscious entrepreneurs are currently the principals of another fine restaurant chain, Travinia Italian Kitchen, with more than a dozen locations, from Destin, Florida to Washington, D.C.

Cox and Craig have invited Pendleton-housed kids to their upscale eatery for more than a decade, so they could escape an austere environment, enjoy a change of scenery, experience the finer things in life and take pleasure in a great meal. Wanting to do more, they initiated that first golf fund-raiser, which is where a semi-disgruntled Mike Williams soon found himself as the reluctant and inexperienced tournament honcho. Safe to say, he's learned to embrace the role.

"Our event isn't based on tournament prizes," explains Williams, "because we give every player in the field a wonderful gift bag. The golf event is just part of an amazing party, with gourmet food prepared on course by professional chefs, things like shrimp and grits, and bacon-wrapped scallops. The new element is the post-tournament concert, which has taken on a life of its own."

Williams and his lifelong friend, fellow area businessman and tournament co-organizer Troy Baldree, felt their event was getting humdrum as a stand-alone golf tournament a decade after its founding. Visiting a John Daly-sponsored charity event in Arkansas for fresh ideas, they made the acquaintance of some A-list musicians, and invited them to Greenville to perform at a post-tournament party. "We didn't want to advertise it for fear they wouldn't show," recalls a chuckling Baldree. Consequently, a fortunate few hundred gathered in the restaurant parking lot got to hear the musicianship of founders and members of iconic bands like Night Ranger, KISS, 38 Special, Chicago, and Starship, jamming together on one stage. Like the evolution of the event itself, the post-tournament concert has only gotten bigger and more popular.

"We now hold our concert, which is called 'Rockin' on the Runway,' in a hangar at the local airport," recounts Williams proudly. "We have a professional production company doing the sound and light. We have welcomed members of the Marshall Tucker Band, Billy Joel's band, and Joan Jett's. We have had four Grammy-winning drummers on stage concurrently."

The musicians, a semi-revolving cast that refer to themselves as "The Magnificent Bastards," make their annual pilgrimage to Greenville to put on an unforgettable show for eight hundred lucky souls, four times as many concert-goers as tournament participants, and do so out of the goodness of their hearts, with just their transportation and accommodations covered.

They, like all those involved in the Arizona's Children's Classic, understand implicitly that it's all about the kids.

For more information visit: www.arizona-open.org

The BASHOF Golf Classic

For a Hall of Fame housed in an airport terminal, the Bay Area Sports Hall of Fame (known by the acronym BASHOF) has a pedigree and legacy that is startling in terms of star power.

Look no further than its inaugural class of 1979, which included Willie Mays, Bill Russell and Joe DiMaggio. Consider that some of the most accomplished and groundbreaking athletes in the history of sport have subsequently been inducted. Football represented by Joe Montana, Jerry Rice, John Elway, John Madden, Steve Young and Ronnie Lott. Tennis stars like Billie Jean King and John McEnroe. Baseball luminaries such as Willie McCovey, Vida Blue and Reggie Jackson. Olympic gold medalists like Mark Spitz, Jonny Moseley, Kristi Yamaguchi and Bob Mathias. Major championship-winning golfers like Tom Watson, Johnny Miller and Ken Venturi.

Not bad, considering it's 'the Hall without a hall,' as VP of Finance and Administration Anthony Savicke explains. "Our founder, Lou Spadia, a former president of the 49ers, wanted to honor the rich legacy of the athletes we venerate who either were born in the Bay Area or played here. But he didn't want to sap resources by having a physical building with upkeep, staff and utilities. So we've always partnered with United Airlines, who provide us terminal space. It's a wonderful arrangement because we get three million visitors a year and don't have the attendant expenses. This leaves us the freedom to allocate our resources elsewhere."

Therein lies the beauty, the delicious irony, of this fine organization. The money

that BASHOF raises through its annual golf event, as well as their enshrinement banquet and sports auction, fund upwards of sixty youth sports organizations every year throughout the eleven counties making up the Bay Area—from San Jose to Marin County, to Oakland and the East Bay. Whether its baseball, football, fencing, swimming, skating, soccer, sailing, running, or any other organized activity, the Hall of Fame makes generous annual donations to purchase much-needed equipment, and keep kids of all ethnicities, abilities and geographies playing, learning and competing.

"We assist thousands of kids every year, and we try to concentrate on underserved areas, or those with lower per-capita incomes," states BASHOF President Kevin O'Brien. "We firmly believe that a sports and athletic background is a great boost to academic and social performance. These young people learn teamwork, discipline, accountability, goal-setting and important life lessons through sports. It is our objective to foster the next generation of responsible, hardworking and diligent youth. They are hopefully developing a lifelong affinity for health, wellness and fitness.

They are learning that not everybody wins, sometimes no matter how hard you try, there are others that are more skillful, or want it more. It is for these reasons, and dozens of others, that we have raised and donated some four million dollars to support more than six hundred separate youth sports programs since 1979."

The golf outing doesn't raise quite as much money for BASHOF as does their annual enshrinement banquet, sprinkled as it is with the glitterati, but it's a key component regardless. First of all, the fundraiser takes over all thirty-six holes at the Olympic Club, one of the city's premier grounds for golf. This venerable facility includes both the Ocean and the Lake Courses, the latter a five-time U.S. Open venue.

Equally impressive was that for over a decade, the late Ken Venturi served as the tournament host. The U.S. Open champion was even better known for the three decades he spent as the lead announcer for CBS golf telecasts, and his presence and support elevated the event, making it a 'must play' for the city's elite. "Ken thought it was a great honor to be inducted into our hall back in 1984," states

O'Brien. "He threw his considerable support behind us, not only for the tournament, but in our ongoing fundraising efforts."

While BASHOF might not have the charm of Cooperstown or the gravitas of Canton, it is highly utilitarian, easily accessible, and offers something new and different every year. "We maintain twenty-five kiosks in the United terminal," continues Savicke, who came onto the job in 2011. "We rotate out four or five plaques a year to make room for the new inductees, and send those plaques to wherever the athlete wants. Many end up at Stanford, AT&T Park, or the Oakland Coliseum." There is one constant amidst the rotation. Joe DiMaggio, an inaugural honoree in the uppermost strata of all inductees, has been represented since day one. "I'll be damned if I would remove him, and send that plaque off to Yankee Stadium," offers Savicke, with a laugh.

The organization is a model of efficiency with only two staff positions and several interns. BASHOF relies heavily on volunteer support. Although their professional staff is a skeleton crew and the actual hall modest in scope, the fundraisers are lavish.

Savicke makes the point that the success of their events relies heavily on the respective venues. For twenty years the golf tournament has been held at the Olympic Club, and the annual enshrinement banquet at the Westin Hotel on Union Square for the past thirty-six years. "We know that to garner the support we need from those who believe in our mission, we have to show them an exceptional time."

That attitude towards hospitality only makes sense, as BASHOF prides itself on an equally exceptional roster of inductees, more than 160, with more enshrined every year. There are undoubtedly a sprinkling of gifted athletes among the thousands assisted by BASHOF's annual

bequests. A select few might end up with a plaque themselves someday, honored at the enshrinement dinner. But all who choose to participate in sports benefit greatly from the organization's profound largesse.

For more information visit:
www.bashof.org

The Beaufort Charities Invitational

In broad terms, there are two types of events- charity events that have a golf component, and golf tournaments giving generously to charity. According to Beaufort Charities Invitational tournament director Christian Sherbert, their long-running affair, now past its fortieth anniversary, is in the latter category. And for that reason as much as any other, it has achieved notable success in recent years.

What began as The Heart Fund back in 1976 morphed into the Beaufort Charities a dozen years later. "We didn't see the logic in sending all the monies raised to the state capital in Columbia," begins board of directors chairman Jimmy Boozer, who has been affiliated with the event for more than thirty years. "We have plenty of need right here in Beaufort County, so that's where we focus our attention."

Up to twenty local-need organizations benefit each year: the local hospital, Habitat for Humanity, an Alzheimer's support group, hospice providers, everything from public schools to senior services.

"It's a balancing act between dispersing the funds we collect via entry fees, and making sure we put on a first-class tournament that keeps people coming back year after year," explains Sherbert, a Beaufort native who's been affiliated with the event for two decades. "It's been a struggle from time to time. When the economy crashed in 2008 we lost more than half the field. We had 250 players at one time, and that number shrunk to 120. But we've built ourselves back up, and part of the reason is we put an emphasis on the competitive nature of the event, so we attract avid, enthusiastic players who want to test themselves year after year."

Many fundraisers are of the casual, "hit and giggle" variety, like an eighteen-hole scramble or captain's choice. Beaufort's iteration, contested in the lush beauty of the Carolina Lowcountry, on gorgeous Fripp Island with the Atlantic Ocean as a backdrop, is a different kettle of fish.

The three-day event consists of nearly a hundred two-man teams, often decked out in matching uniforms, playing best ball over thirty-six holes. "Our players want to feel the same nerves on the first tee when they get introduced as the professionals they admire on television do every week on the PGA Tour," continues Sherbert, a former mini-tour player himself. "That's why they return annually, and the beauty is that longstanding relationships and partnerships get formed here. We have surgeons who partner up with electricians, judges who play with landscapers, lawyers teaming up with a cop or fireman. Golf, and by association our event, is the great equalizer."

It's no simple thing to raise big money is a sleepy seaside town of twelve thousand. While big city events might get sponsors forking over half a million, this event has rarely seen an individual sponsor pay as much as five thousand dollars. But it's a big deal nonetheless, with local media coverage, live radio feeds, and teams from Atlanta, Greenville, Charlotte, Columbia and other points on the compass coming to one of the loveliest locales in the southeast. Slow and steady wins the race, though. The Beaufort Charities has raised in excess of $800,000 for their local agencies over the years. Explaining the recent emphasis on producing a competitive event, attractive to both strong and handicap golfers, Sherbert continues: "There are a thousand places you can write a check. But finding a fun, lively and competitive event like ours isn't so easy. By emphasizing the golf itself, we attract a loyal clientele, they tell their buddies, and overall we can do more for our causes in need every year."

It's not just the not-for-profits receiving annual checks that benefit. Because of the unique quality of the Lowcountry, and the fact that many teams come from out of the area, year after year local artists are engaged by the tournament committee to produce commemorative paintings, drawings and posters as prizes. "The artistic community is a tremendous asset to Beaufort," states Sherbert, a realtor by profession. "We take pride in hiring them to produce original artwork for our event, and the framings we distribute are always a big hit."

The PGA Tour comes to Hilton Head Island every April, and the Heritage Tournament is consistently rated among the players' favorites. They relax and unwind with their wives and families, biking and beaching while not on course. Though driving the two-lane byways from Fripp to the south end of Hilton Head would take some ninety minutes, the fact is that as the crow flies (or the speedboat rumbles) the islands are barely fifteen miles apart. "There's probably not many three-day charity golf events where the wives encourage their husbands to play," offers Jimmy Boozer with a laugh. "But ours is the exception I guess. They come as a family, maybe rent a beach house with other friends, and have a great time."

"I was watching The Heritage on Hilton Head one year," concludes Sherbert, serving as the twelfth tournament chairman of the Beaufort Charities Invitational. "I thought it was so cool that Craig Stadler, the former Masters champion who played the Heritage dozens of times, was in the gallery watching his son, Kevin. Then at our event a few weeks later, I am introducing two father-and-son teams on the first tee, playing together!"

"The economy has its ups and downs, golf continues to diminish nationwide, but I'm confident we will always persevere. Over time we have developed these deep family bonds, fathers and sons together with moms and wives and kids. They love coming to Fripp, they love our event, and the fact that they support our many needy agencies so generously with their entry fees is the icing on the cake."

For more information visit: www.BeaufortCharities.org

Bighorn Institute Golf Classic

The greatness of a nation and its moral progress can be judged by the way its animals are treated. - Mahatma Gandhi

The domino effect. That is likely the single most compelling reason to protect the population of Peninsular desert bighorn sheep, an endangered species of less than a thousand found in and around the desert of Palm Springs, California.

"What's important to understand is that bighorn are considered an 'umbrella species.' When they are protected, then the lands they inhabit, the vegetation they eat, the smaller mammals and critters that live in that same habitat, are also protected." So begins Aimee Byard, a biologist and associate director of Bighorn Institute. "As it is their critical habitat has been drastically reduced from 800,000 acres down to 400,000 acres. We need to protect what's left to insure that the bighorn can thrive into the future."

Not all bighorn are endangered. For example, the Rocky Mountain bighorn number more than thirty thousand, due in some part because they thrive at high elevation, around ten thousand feet above sea level, and their habitat doesn't generally conflict with where mankind tends to live. But the Peninsular bighorn's preferred habitat is much lower, about four thousand feet and below, and consequently they occupy the same turf as those building second homes or choosing to retire in the Coachella Valley, Riverside County and greater Palm Springs. Therein lies the conflict.

"Our goal is to educate and enlighten people. Knowledge is the key," explains James DeForge, the executive director of the Bighorn Institute. "The more knowledge scientists gather the better they can understand and fight deadly diseases. By the same token, the more knowledge we can spread regarding the importance of keeping these bighorn a viable species, the better it will be for all living things, humans and animals."

"We consider ourselves caretakers," continues DeForge, whose involvement dates to the founding of the organization in 1982. He originally came to the region as part of a group of biologists who discovered that the bighorn lambs at that time were dying in disproportionate numbers due to bacterial pneumonia caused by viruses. The institute formed a captive breeding program from rehabilitated animals and it is now recognized as a federal recovery facility. "It can't always be about man, because that inevitably leads to dirty air, dirty water and a polluted environment. All species are important, and when a species disappears, it's often the mark of a society moving in the wrong direction."

As so many things do, the conservation movement revolves around money. "Because this animal is endangered, it usually does not benefit from the hundreds of thousands of dollars contributed by hunter conservation groups. As a result, Peninsular bighorn sometimes fly under the radar since they don't bring state agencies money. But, you cannot put a price tag or a monetary value on every species to define its worth." By direct contrast, DeForge points out that there are now more deer in the nation than when the Pilgrims came ashore at Plymouth Rock nearly four hundred years ago. "There's a concerted effort to keep the deer population robust, and the beginning of deer hunting season feels like Christmas for those who love to hunt and bag a buck."

Bagging bucks of the other kind to keep the institute afloat is part of the staff's directive, as much as they wish they could concentrate their efforts on research and captive breeding alone. Awareness of the cause and keeping funds flowing are on-

going battles. "Mankind is predisposed to support causes that benefit themselves," states Byard, a biologist by training. "It's a challenge to emphasize how important this research really is. We monitor several hundred bighorn in our area, and are gratified that we were able to repopulate two separate herds, or subgroups, that were in danger of dying out completely; we have released approximately 130 bighorn into the wild since 1985, all with private funds. We are very pleased we were able to expand a herd from four to twenty five. Our focus is that gray area where man and the sheep population overlap, which is mostly in the foothills around Palm Springs."

The institute relies on private funding almost exclusively, and their annual golf event, now nearing its thirtieth anniversary, is an integral component of their mission. At least a quarter of their annual operating budget, and sometimes as much as fifty percent, comes from the proceeds of their fundraising tournament. The institute was fortunate to find Dave Stockton as an advocate, organizer, and what the biologists consider to be the backbone of their golf fundraiser since the very beginning.

Speaking of the two-time major champion and former Ryder Cup captain, DeForge explains, "as an avid hunter, Dave has a passion for wildlife and a great conservation ethic. And because he has done so many hundreds of corporate golf outings in his long career, he really knows the right way to run a high-end golf event. It's been very serendipitous to have him on our board for such a long time."

Stockton's success as a golf professional is mirrored by equally impressive resumes in other fields of endeavor by current and former board members. Powerful business leaders, successful real estate developers, doctors, scientists and all manner of high achievers have found their way onto the board, which at one time included former President Gerald Ford.

It's doubtful that even President Ford, as much as he loved golf, could attract the caliber of golfers that Stockton has brought to the desert every year to take part in the fundraiser and assist with the clinics. Luminaries like Lee Trevino, Annika Sorenstam, Al Geiberger, and Stockton's sons, Dave Jr. and Ron, have been or are regular participants.

Held at the exclusive and dramatic Stone Eagle Club, hallmarked by rugged boulder outcroppings and jaw-dropping long views of the valley, the tournament field is limited to little more than seventy participants to ensure that all the patrons enjoy a premium experience. Despite her role as chief tournament organizer, Aimee Byard has little interest in playing golf herself. "I've tried it, but honestly, I prefer team sports," she concludes with a chuckle. "That way there are others to blame after a mistake."

Byard, DeForge, and the many zealous proponents of the Bighorn Institute realize that taking the bighorn sheep population for granted, and not advocating on behalf of these animals, would also be a major mistake.

Bighorn Institute

For more information visit: www.bighorninstitute.org

The Bill Sugra Memorial Fund

The final time Bill and El Sugra laid eyes on their son Bill Jr. was shortly after his 30th birthday, in early August of 2001. "He was so solicitous of us, he always met us, then returned us to the Port Authority station in Manhattan, even though we were perfectly capable," recalls his mother. "But that was our Billy. He was a loving, caring individual, and the best son you could hope for. For some reason, after he dropped us off I started to cry as he walked away."

Call it a mother's intuition. Little more than a month later, Bill was gone. A victim of the terrorist attacks on the World Trade Center, he was one of seven hundred Cantor-Fitzgerald employees who perished that dreadful day. He was ensconced in his 103rd floor office in the north tower when the first jetliner made impact some ten floors below. "We had spoken the night before, on the 10th," El relates tearfully. "He was upset that one of his IT department colleagues had been terminated that day, despite the fact he had more tenure than Bill. Losing his job was the luckiest thing that ever happened to that man, because he wasn't in the tower the next morning. But Billy was."

El was called from her elementary school classroom to the administrative office that morning. Bill, a plumber, was told to head to the school, and thought something had happened to his wife. A TV in the custodian's office allowed Bill to monitor the situation as it unfolded, but El never looked. To this day, she has never viewed a moment of the carnage. "I was just pacing and praying," relates the longtime educator.

The days and weeks that followed were numbing to Bill, El and their daughter Tracy. Their Allentown, Pennsylvania home was filled with neighbors, friends, co-workers, grade-schoolers, sympathizers, fellow parishioners, clergy, political emissaries and other well-meaning individuals

who inundated them with visits, food, and words of comfort. "I just wanted to be alone in my room, not see or talk to anyone," states El, "but the constant stream of visitors forced me out of my shell, made me interact, which helped the grieving process."

The genesis of the Bill Sugra Memorial Fund was the annual St. Thomas More Catholic Church Walk-A-Thon, which takes place every October. "About a month after 9/11, these walking fundraisers were rerouted by our house," recalls Bill Sr., who like his wife is a lifelong resident of Allentown. "Bill and Tracy had walked in it numerous times, and in 2001, a well-meaning middle school kid, who obviously wasn't completely aware of the tragedy's scope, suggested to our priest that the monies raised be donated to us, to help with our son's hospital bills."

A thousand walkers paraded by the house that day to honor the Sugra Family, stopping to recite poems and sing the national anthem, with local media providing full coverage. Explains Tracy, "It became a memorial walk for my brother Bill, and instead of the normal $45,000 raised, that year it was $75,000."

Over the weeks there were casseroles, condolence cards and flowers galore, but the family also received dozens of unsolicited checks from well-wishers throughout the region. As the patriarch explains, "at that time, people just wanted to do more. Recall how people were flying American flags, both at their homes and on their car antennas. Bill's senseless death just struck a chord in our city, is the best way I can explain it."

Despite their religious faith, the Sugras didn't want to just support Catholic charities. "Our son was deeply caring of those less fortunate," explains El. "He would buy coffee for the homeless on cold days as he walked to work, was always there for a friend in need, had a kind word for his younger sister, things of that nature. With this windfall we wanted to support a wide range of charities across the spectrum. We wanted to create an endowment that would last for decades, and not just distribute it in one fell swoop."

A family friend had a business associate who ran golf tournaments, and suggested one as an ongoing fundraiser. The Bill Sugra Memorial Golf Outing debuted in 2002, and has since distributed nearly half a million dollars to more than seventy worthwhile organizations. It's important to note that the sole means of funding the foundation comes through the proceeds of the annual golf event.

Their underlying philosophy is to encourage, support and assist the needy and disadvantaged to improve their lives during times of difficulty, regardless of location, race, religion, or gender. The monies distributed annually assist children, those with special needs, seniors and the underprivileged.

The Sugras began running the event themselves after about five years. "By cutting out the management company fees it was a way for us to raise more money," explains Bill, who was a twice-a-week golfer for many years.

The low-key Sugra Memorial will never be mistaken for a celebrity tournament, but there is one A-list star who is an ardent supporter and serves as the title sponsor.

One of Bill's high school classmates was knockout actress Christine Taylor, blonde and beautiful, who is married to one of Hollywood's biggest names, Ben Stiller. Though they've never actually attended, perhaps someday Zoolander himself, clad in his trademark leopard skin golf slacks, will stroll the fairways of Green Pond Country Club, the perpetual host of this heartfelt event.

In 2002, on what would have been his 31st birthday the Sugras got a call from New York. Some of Bill's remains had finally been located. "I was a hysterical mess," recalls El. "But Monsignor Murphy from our church, who was going to dinner with us that evening to commemorate Bill's life, reassured us it was a sign from him, letting us know he was OK, he loved us, and to go on with our lives. I took great comfort in that."

There were nearly 3,000 victims of 9/11, all remembered tenderly by their family, friends and neighbors. Thanks to the Bill Sugra Memorial Golf Outing, each summer more than 150 kindly Pennsylvanians take sticks in hand to celebrate a life well lived, but cut well short, remembering a man destined for great things, who always tried to do good.

For more information visit:
www.billsugramemorialfund.org

The Billy Frank Jr. Golf Classic

If you are a staunch environmentalist, a Native American, or someone who resides in the Pacific Northwest, there's a chance you might be familiar with Salmon Defense. But most of the rest of the nation has no clue that this organization exists, or about the inspiring work they do to make sure the salmon keep swimming. With their work, salmon remain a vital part of the ecosystem and an integral component of life for untold thousands of Native Americans in and around Puget Sound in Washington State.

As for the tournament's namesake, Billy Frank Jr. is a legendary name in the world of Native Americans, and no individual worked harder to make Salmon Defense a viable and effective organization. A Nisqually tribal member, Frank was arrested more than fifty times during his life, as he insisted on his right to fish, hunt and gather shellfish that were granted to his and other tribes in the mid-1850s via treaties with the U.S. government. He also served as chairman of the Northwest Indian Fisheries Commission for more than thirty years. Frank was so highly regarded as a transformative figure that when he passed in 2014, government flags in Washington State flew at half mast. Among the many accolades and awards he received during his long career as an advocate for native rights was the Albert Schweitzer Prize for Humanitarianism. Frank was in esteemed company, considering other Schweitzer honorees include Desmond Tutu, C. Everett Koop, Norman Cousins

and Jimmy Carter.

There are 562 different Native American tribes in the U.S. There are twenty-nine federally recognized tribes in Washington, twenty of which are treaty tribes, which have entered into various treaties with the government. It was these twenty tribes, in conjunction with some others throughout the region, who created Salmon Defense. Their mission is to protect and defend salmon and their habitats in the Pacific Northwest.

"It is hard to overestimate how essential salmon are to tribes throughout the region," explains Fran Wilshusen, the executive director of Salmon Defense. She has been with the organization since it was founded in 2003, and been serving in various environmental and natural resource management capacities for some thirty years. "It is more than just food or sustenance. It is part of their culture, their lifeways, their very makeup. In some ways it is who they are." Defending salmon by definition means protecting the waterways and the environment. Hunting elk and deer, gathering plants and herbs for medicine and craftwork, and fishing are cultural traditions. Tribes are staunch advocates of their right to carry on their ways of life. "Salmon is essential to the health of these communities," offers the executive director.

Advocate. Litigate. Educate. These are the tenets of Salmon Defense. They advocate for clean and flowing water, oppose dams, and actively campaign for the healthiest habitat. Litigation is a last resort, but if need be the group will take legal steps to ensure that that clean and cool water that salmon need to live in and spawn isn't compromised or diverted. They educate by producing information-packed DVDs and visiting schools to explain the significance of their mission. Tribal Voices Archive is an additional project. They record oral histories from elders who explain life and connection to place and its resources, like salmon, critical to tribal traditions since time immemorial.

All of these projects are funded in part by their annual golf tournament, where participants are urged to "swing a club, save a salmon." Up to half of their operation budget comes from the golf event. "It's more than just a golf tournament," offers Wilshusen. "It's a day for various tribal leaders and other partners and friends to gather for a day of golf, combining fun and fundraising to protect salmon and the habitats on which they depend."

It's also a festive day, with so many of the tribes contributing generously for the enjoyment of the gathering. It begins with the Jamestown S'Kllalam tribe, who donate their lovely golf course, The Cedars at Dungeness, for the entire day. The Muckleshoot Tribe and the Kongsgaard Goldman Foundation sponsor the jacket that each player receives at the tournament. These jackets have become the trademark attire of this event and are seen being worn throughout the year, reminding people of the ongoing work and their commitment to the region's salmon. Probably eighty percent of the players are Native Americans, a very impressive turnout that beautifully illustrates how vital the cause is to the various tribes. Nobody goes hungry as they're swinging clubs and saving salmon. The Squaxin Island tribe's Salish Seafood Company grills oysters with bleu cheese and bacon on the first tee all day long; cholesterol be damned, as this tee is understandably one of the most popular gathering spots on the course.

For most people, the only consideration they give salmon is whether to buy it farm-raised or wild. They'll order smoked salmon with cream cheese on a bagel, or maybe have salmon sushi at a Japanese restaurant. Luckily for the rest of us, there are tribes working tirelessly like the good folks at Salmon Defense, embodied by the decades of advocacy provided by the late Billy Frank, Jr., and equally committed current board members like Bob Whitener, Bob Kelly, Lorraine Loomis, Fawn Sharp and Ron Allen. They realize that the fish is more than a dietary staple and that its ongoing presence is vital for both the human and animal populations that depend on its continued viability.

For more information
visit: www.salmondefense.org

Bobby Nichols
Fiddlesticks Charity Foundation

If someone mentioned that more than two-thirds of a sizeable community got behind the same charitable effort every year, two out of every three residents gave their time, effort and money, a skeptic might not believe such across-the-board altruism exists. Their cynical reply might be "Fiddlesticks!" How right they would be.

Fiddlesticks Country Club in Fort Myers, Florida is a diverse community with over five hundred homes. Golf is an important part of the landscape, and with two championship courses the club enjoys one of the lowest course densities in golf-loving southwest Florida.

However there is also a plethora of community-minded and charitably inclined residents who have banded together to create and sustain one of the most successful charity events in the state if not the country.

Bobby Nichols is a founding member of the club, and could theoretically keep the club championship trophy in perpetuity if he were inclined. Fortunately for his fellow members, Nichols, who won a dozen times on the PGA Tour including the 1964 PGA Championship, prefers to focus on his charitable efforts. He picked the right community in which to do so.

"Fiddlesticks members come together to make a difference in this community," states Nichols, who finished second and third, in the Masters and U.S. Open respectively, in addition to his PGA Championship win. "Their dedication to the world outside the gates is admirable and has changed the lives of so many children in need."

In 2002 the Bobby Nichols-Fiddlesticks Charity Foundation was formed. The non-profit's mission was to help abused and at-risk children in Southwest Florida, and the cause resonated deeply and immediately with his many friends and neighbors.

"I think the members have realized their good fortune in moving to Fiddlesticks and living in this paradise," offers Earl Holland, a founding member of the club, who serves as chairman of the charitable foundation. "Speaking for myself, this community has opened up a world of activities and friendships that have exceeded my imagination. Many of us wanted something more, something that ran deeper, that touched the soul, which left a mark, something where the community could come together and make a difference in the lives of the many children in jeopardy. These are some of the reasons the Foundation has enjoyed this success."

The Bobby Nichols-Fiddlesticks Charity Foundation focuses their efforts on three local agencies in the Fort Meyers area, all of which advocate for at-risk children. Children's Advocacy Center, Abuse Counseling and Treatment, and Blessings in a Backpack are the beneficiaries and good stewards of the monies donated to their organizations, which is astonishingly in excess of seven million dollars.

Each agency focuses on a different aspect of the mission to improve the lives of disadvantaged kids. The Children's Advocacy Center endeavors to prevent crisis situations. The Abuse Counseling and Treatment Center works with families needing a shelter during a state of emergency. Finally, Blessings in a Backpack provides weekend meals for underprivileged children at two Title One local elementary schools.

Jill Turner is the CEO of the Children's Advocacy Center. She is both amazed at the club's enthusiasm and forever grateful for the largesse provided to her organization. "We are able to help more than four thousand children a year, who are all better off because of Fiddlesticks."

Abuse Counseling and Treatment CEO

Jennifer Benton says that "Knowing you can provide safe shelter, counseling and support services to a child that has been abused or watched a loved one being abused, is our number one priority. Without the foundation's funding, many children would be left without hope and the help they so desperately need."

Blessings in a Backpack provides weekend nourishment for hundreds of local elementary students who would otherwise be hungry when school meals are not provided. The backpack gives them nourishment so they return to school on Monday eager and ready to learn. Some families have been found to only have the backpack of food in their home on the weekends. The program has enabled outreach and food bank programs to intervene.

Many or most charity golf events are one-day affairs. Some of the bigger ones include a dinner the evening prior. But Fiddlesticks takes an entire long weekend to raise funds, promote awareness, and have a joyous time while doing so. For many members, the Nichols Cup Weekend festivities are the highlight of the year.

The tournament weekend has evolved to include a Friday night gathering to celebrate friendship and community. Saturday features a tennis tournament, children's walk-a-thon and an evening party and raffle to complete the day. Sunday's highlight is a gala auction and Monday is the golf tournament itself. The Fiddlesticks membership comes together to bring this weekend to life with over four hundred volunteers working tirelessly on every detail. Both championship golf courses are at capacity on President's Day as nearly five hundred individuals, including many well-known professionals, come together as players and spectators for this grand event. Besides the serious fundraising, it's a weekend of awareness, camaraderie, togetherness and fun for the entire community.

While many take part, the backbone of the organization is a group called the Pipers. These are Fiddlesticks members that donate money to the mission every year and are an integral part of the charity event weekend. The Pipers truly stitch the fabric of the inspirational weekend, and nearly every Fiddlesticks household participates. Not only does their annual membership fee help fund the chosen charities, but many Pipers also go out of their way to solicit additional donations from the surrounding community, all of which go directly to the charities. Thanks to the generosity of the event sponsors and the financial support of the foundation's board of directors, all costs associated with the weekend are absorbed.

The weekend attracts marquee names from the world of sports and professional golf in addition to the Pipers and sponsors. Over the years luminaries like baseball's Johnny Bench and Dwight Evans, and hockey's Bobby Orr have participated. Golf stars such as Fuzzy Zoeller, Lanny Wadkins, Loren Roberts, Peter Jacobson, Chip Beck, Fulton Allem, Andy Bean, Lou Graham, Jerry Heard, Nolan Henke, David Mobley, Dan Pohl, Bob Toski, Scott Hoch, Tony Jacklin, Larry Laoretti, Wayne Levi, Mark Lye, Larry Ziegler and local product George McNeill, who is a member of Fiddlesticks,

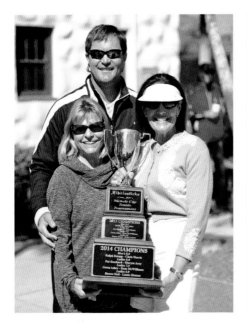

have lent their considerable cachet to the event.

The community was humbled by recent recognition of their efforts, including being presented the Key to the City in October 2014 by the Mayor of Fort Myers and most recently, the 2015 Florida Communities of Excellence Award in civic volunteerism and advocacy by Volunteer Florida.

All of this spirit goes beyond the Bobby Nichols-Fiddlesticks Charity Foundation. The yearly United Way campaign and golf tournament is also orchestrated by the membership, and raises over $200,000 annually. There is also Fiddlesticks Cares, the community's own volunteer organization, where members can select the charity that's right for them. It can be as an individual, or a group of members gathering together for larger projects. Members within this community glean the same level of satisfaction from helping others as they do in enjoying the top-notch amenities at the club. An active tennis community, world-class fitness, spa and yoga facilities, and a new cabana and pool area are all important parts of the overall package.

This unusual balance of living and giving, fun and dedicated volunteerism, has become the cornerstone of the community and what makes Fiddlesticks a one-of-a-kind locale. "I've seen and played golf at more wonderful places then I can re-member," concludes Bobby Nichols. "There is nowhere I would rather live and play than right here in Fort Myers, with the many caring members of Fiddlesticks."

For more information visit: www.nicholscup.org

Building Homes for Heroes

Some of the events featured in this book have ambiguous titles. Most readers couldn't guess what the Cragmont, Corvias Foundation or the Healing Place, to give but three examples, actually represent. Not the case with Building Homes for Heroes, one of the most straightforward (not to mention one of the noblest) causes chronicled within these pages.

This national not-for-profit, non-partisan foundation can be described as a wonderful amalgamation of Wounded Warriors and Habitat for Humanity. They support courageous men and women who have been severely injured during the wars in Iraq or Afghanistan by giving them mortgage-free homes.

The organization was founded by New Yorker Andy Pujol, one of thousands of Ground Zero volunteers who aided the search-and-rescue efforts at the World Trade Center following the traumatic events of 9/11. Recalling that day, Pujol says, "I took a rest, took off my mask and helmet, and sat there with tears in my eyes from what I was witnessing. I wanted to do something more for my country: something that was patriotic, something that made a difference."

Several years passed before the right opportunity presented itself. One fortuitous day Pujol was listening to the radio when he heard a genuine American hero—a wounded war veteran—speaking poignantly about his combat experiences and his willingness to carry on. After hearing him promote an event to support soldiers who sacrificed so valiantly for our nation, Pujol did more than donate and volunteer. He took the next step and launched a more meaningful cause: Building Homes for Heroes.

Pujol clearly understood the lure of building a place to call home for those who loyally gave

service. In one recent survey, nearly ninety percent of veterans said owning a home made them feel safer by providing them with a strong sense of financial security and community. Yet home ownership has been tantalizingly out of reach. Very few veterans, let alone badly injured ones, have the financial resources to fully participate in the American dream of homeownership.

"Our nation's veterans often face unimaginable obstacles, including severe physical injuries, PTSD, and joblessness," Pujol says. "With the gifting of a home, we are changing and rebuilding lives. We are making our communities and country a better place. Most of all, we are providing hope and happiness and better preparing our veterans and their families for the many challenges that lie ahead."

The first work by Building Homes for Heroes was for a veteran outside of Gainesville, Florida, who was paralyzed from the neck down. Many other customized homes followed, including special adapted homes for U.S. Army Sergeant Joel Tavera, who has endured nearly one hundred surgeries, for an Air Force Master Sergeant who lost three limbs while assessing the damage of an IED explosion, for an Army Corporal who was forced to undergo two leg amputations above the knee after bravely serving in Afghanistan's "Valley of Death," and for dozens of others who sacrificed their well-being for our freedom. These are just a few example of the hundred-plus homes the organization has provided for our deserving veterans.

A recurring theme throughout this book is that the financial crisis that beset the nation and turned the housing market upside down in 2008 and 2009 was a severe impediment for non-profits in their growth plans. Surprisingly, the same crisis was a tremendous boon to Building Homes for Heroes.

The number of foreclosed properties on the market exploded, and Building Homes for Heroes partnered with Chase Bank to acquire them. "They had literally thousands of real estate foreclosures nationwide," explains Pujol. "Instead of

watching and waiting until the economy improved, the bank became proactive. Chase plans on donating a thousand homes to a few handpicked non-profits, while supporting career transition throughout their own financial institution and at over 170 coalition companies for more than 200,000 veterans."

As a result of the bank's generosity, Building Homes for Heroes began making modifications to the foreclosed homes that were donated in addition to building homes from the ground up. After taking receivership, the bank repaired the homes, painted them, replaced fixtures, and made them look almost as good as new. Then Building Homes for Heroes took over.

"Wounded veterans have special needs that go above and beyond the general homeowner. So where necessary, we widen doors and hallways, install ramps and lifts, and modify kitchens and bathrooms to make them home handicap accessible," Pujol explains.

"When wheelchair, reach and related accessibility concerns become an issue, we install technology that allows doors to open and close automatically, cabinets to lower electronically, and heating/air conditioning and lighting to be electronically adjusted. When PTSD is a worry, we provide soothing enhancements through sight and sound softening features: pavers and pergolas, gurgling fountains, and streams of running water designed to help with ringing in the ears, tinnitus and anxiety."

The organization has recently introduced additional programs for veterans, such as financial planning services, family funding, and emergency support. It's all designed to provide new homeowners with the support and insight they need to keep up with home expenses, and plan successfully for the future.

Their Long Island-based golf tournament has been instrumental in the organization's rapid growth. "It was our first-ever fundraising event and continues to reach new heights each year," offers Chad Gottlieb, a key executive in the organization.

"Many are inspired by the stories shared by an ever-growing number of home recipients. Hundreds of supporters attend the dinner each year. So many contractors, companies and individuals embrace the organization after attending the tournament."

Attendees are sometimes moved to tears when they came face-to-face with the valiant men and women who so honorably fought for our country and suffered catastrophic injuries such as dismemberment, blindness, or disfiguring wounds during the course of their multiple tours of duty. Many want to know how they can also make a meaningful difference.

One of these advocates was Jason Evanchik, an upper level executive with PVH Corp., which owns Calvin Klein, Van Heusen, Tommy Hilfiger and many other companies. After attending a Building Homes for Heroes golf event, he was motivated to initiate a sister tournament in New Jersey.

"I've known and admired Andy for about fifteen years," Evanchik says. "As our friendship grew, he invited me to be more involved with Building Homes for Heroes. At first, I assisted him by bringing together golfers and potential supporters. It wasn't long thereafter that we decided to build an equally passionate event in New Jersey. In many ways, we compete with one another in a meaningful manner to help more of our nation's hopeful veterans. The cause has become very personal for me and my wife, our family and friends. So much so that we picnic with our military guests at our home prior to our event so that we really get to know them and hear their stories. When we bring them to the outing, they play golf if possible, chat and speak with others, and inspire all."

Due in large part to the financial acumen of Pujol, a successful freight-forwarder who takes no compensation from the non-profit he founded, Building Homes for Heroes has enjoyed both phenomenal growth and efficiency. Their assets grow steadily, as does the percentage of funds they devote to the cause. Impressive from the get-go at eighty-seven percent efficiency, they soon moved to ninety-three, then to nearly ninety-five, meaning only a nickel of every dollar taken in is diverted from their mission.

Every hero deserves a home, and Building Homes for Heroes will continue to make a memorable difference towards ensuring that veterans are defined by their accomplishments and activities, not their injuries and disabilities. They're not just building homes, they're rebuilding lives.

For more information
visit: www.buildinghomesforheroes.org

The JEHH Memorial Golf Tournament

In the wide range of human emotional responses, there can be nothing more disparate, nor more devastating.

The Harrington family of Bernardston, Massachusetts were hightailing it to the hospital in nearby Springfield in the spring of 2010. They were excited to welcome sister Jill's firstborn child into the world. A new cousin and a new grandchild would be coming into the family fold. But instead of balloons and baby blankets, the news they received was beyond crushing. In excruciating pain, opened up for a caesarean section, the thirty-two-year-old newlywed died in childbirth. The autopsy revealed stage four colon cancer, and her baby son Chase, while technically not a stillborn, died shortly thereafter. Could there be a crueler, more pitiless circumstance?

"My wife and I drove to the hospital with big smiles on our faces," recalls her younger brother Kevin. "We were thrilled for our child to have a new cousin. We couldn't believe what transpired when we arrived; it was beyond overwhelming, it was freakish. As bad as anything else was having to call my brother Adam, who was playing professional basketball in Croatia. Giving him that news was the hardest thing I've ever had to do."

Perhaps as a reflex action to their ongoing grief, Kevin and Adam rallied quickly and decisively. Within two month's time they had organized and executed a charity golf event for nearly one hundred and fifty, including a dinner gala with a hundred more. The Harrington brothers attributed that initial turnout as much to pity and shock as anything else, but they were determined to remember the vibrant legacy of how Jill had lived life to the fullest, and not dwell on the merciless, though mercifully quick, way she died. Thus began the JEHH Memorial Fund, more commonly referred to as Chase Your Dreams Now, not

only to commemorate the name of their infant nephew who barely drew a breath, but to celebrate the way Jill lived life.

States Adam, who enjoyed a decade-long career as a professional basketball player, "people grieve in different ways, and we decided to be super positive. We aren't glossing over Jill's death, but instead of focusing on how she died, and funnel money towards colon cancer research, we wanted to honor her life and spirit and help other kids chase their own dreams. We don't focus on what she died from, but what she lived for."

"Jill was an amazing woman, and when I think of her, which I do daily, I don't think about those final hours. I think about how she lived those thirty-two years, and what an amazing life force she had," continues Kevin. "I think that after the initial wave of fundraising ran its course we've been able to sustain things because of the rich way she lived."

Jill had followed her brother Adam to Dallas

after he was drafted to play for the NBA's Mavericks. The family jokes that Jill lasted much longer in Big D than her brother, as she became billionaire owner Mark Cuban's personal assistant. Some years later she went to New York for a job at the NBA home office. She was instrumental in facilitating legends events with some of the league's biggest names during all-star weekend, the playoffs and the finals. "She used to say 'the suite life was a sweet life,' which made us laugh," recalls Kevin. "She was mingling with some of the greatest players in league history."

Despite a career rubbing elbows with the athletic elite, it was an anonymous ski instructor who caught Jill's fancy. "She was visiting us one weekend in Massachusetts, and at age thirty decided to take her first ski lesson," recalls Kevin. Asked how skiing wasn't a factor while growing up in a town adjacent to the Vermont border, Kevin Harrington offers a simple response. Alluding to his brother's college years as a Division I player, his own in Division II and their sister's single year of Division III ball, he states simply, "we were a basketball family."

Jill decided to leave Gotham and

settle in the quietude of the Green Mountains with her new husband, Joe Hanzalik, the ski school director at Mount Snow in southern Vermont. True to form, Jill quickly landed a plum corporate job in the nearby town of Brattleboro. This was no easy feat, as the quaint former mill town with a population of twelve thousand is not exactly known as a center of commerce.

With a quarter-million dollars raised since 2010, the JEHH Memorial Fund makes a wide range of grants. They help with travel expenses to get dance or cheerleading teams to far-off competitions. They've sent a school group on a mega-field trip to the Grand Canyon. They will buy underfunded afterschool programs basketballs, tennis rackets and other sports equipment so they might unlock undiscovered athletic potential. They attempt to incentivize and motivate young people, by providing matching grants to whatever funds these schools or clubs can raise on their own.

To date, their flagship project is the complete refurbishment of the town basketball court in the main park in Bernardston. "It was dilapidated and barely usable," relates Kevin. "Now it's a point of pride for everyone in town, and is in constant use with scores of happy, active kids on a daily basis."

The Harrington family is raising funds through four channels. A five-kilometer run, a gala dinner and auction preceding the golf tournament, the tournament itself, and a 'give back' event where they host ten local high school basketball teams. Not only do they provide niceties and special touches to reveal a glimpse of what might await them should they pursue their basketball dreams beyond high school, but they also make a generous contribution to each school's athletic department.

Always willing to chase her own dreams, the Brothers Harrington will persist in honoring their sister Jill's legacy. Their fundraising efforts will continue unabated, as they endeavor to help motivated and adventurous kids in New England and beyond chase their own dreams. Now, and in the future.

For more information visit: www.chaseyourdreamsnow.org

The Orion Classic

South Dakota's most famous landmark is indisputably Mount Rushmore, with its magnificent six-story carvings of Washington, Jefferson, Roosevelt and Lincoln. Despite the fact that it took the sculptor nearly fifteen years to create, the total cost of the project was just a million dollars. Of course, it's now considered priceless.

The same can be said for the wonderful work being done by Children's Home Society of South Dakota. One cannot put a dollar figure on the vital nature of their task, which is not easy to describe in a sentence or two because this multifaceted organization offers dozens of different services to a wide range of South Dakotans. But suffice it to say they offer help, shelter, counseling and comfort to many thousands of abused, neglected and otherwise compromised women and children in every corner of this vast, sparsely populated state. What could be more priceless than that?

The first Children's Home Society commenced operations in Chicago in 1883. The concept quickly spread to over thirty states, and into South Dakota just a decade later, in 1893. The core mission of the organization was originally to serve as an orphanage. As the concept of the orphanage gave way to individual foster care in the 1950s and 60s, the focus of these various Children's

Home Societies started to shift. "We support, protect and enhance the lives of children, women and families. Our primary focus is domestic violence and child abuse." So begins Rick Weber, the development director of the organization's charitable arm, known as Children's Home Foundation.

Children's Home Society of South Dakota is so diverse, with numerous programs in varying locations, that the best way to get a handle on its ubiquity is through a couple of hard numbers. The organization has an eighteen million dollar budget, 360 employees and many hundreds of volunteers.

Many of their primary facilities are located in Sioux Falls, the most populous city in South Dakota, which is in the southeast portion of the state, not far from the Iowa and Minnesota borders. The Sioux Falls Children's Home is one of the organization's main sites, and Black Hills Children's Home is in the western portion of the state, more than three hundred miles away. They also have foster

care and adoption through their community-based services located in both Rapid City and Sioux Falls.

The Children's Inn in Sioux Falls is another integral facility, and a critical part of their services. It's an emergency shelter for victims of domestic violence and child abuse. Some shelters have undisclosed locations, but not in this case. "We offer tight security, so only those who need to be here can access the facility," offers Rick Weber. "But to best assist our clientele we feel we need to be easy to locate. In many cases we have women and children driving significant distances to get here, so we want to make it as easy as we can for them."

Therein lies one of the major challenges facing Children's Home Society of South Dakota: distance. It's a rural, agrarian state, with a surfeit of small towns, and great expanses of roads and highways separating one pocket of civilization from the next. Accessing the services offered by the organization requires no small effort, despite their presence in different areas of the state. "Getting kids and families to our facilities isn't always easy or convenient, and ongoing therapy and follow up visits are also challenging," offers Tom Roberts, the event coordinator for the Orion Classic golf fundraiser.

It's virtually impossible to gauge how many people are touched by the organization annually. Some kids might come in for a two hour forensic interview, others might live on site for a year or more. But it's no stretch to say the number of individuals served is in the thousands. Particularly in the western portion of the

state, the Native American population is sizable. While there are other organizations specifically geared to serve the tribes, Children's Home Society does have a cultural relations advisor who works with the Native American children in their care.

They have 115 residential treatment beds, and some stays become very extensive. "Some children have deep-seated psychological and emotional issues, which require long term care by our counseling staff," offers Deb Moritz, another longtime staff member.

Another important part of their mission is finding foster and adoptive families for children who are unable to return to their birth parents. In addition to recruitment there is training, counseling and follow-up requirements. "We specialize in helping very young children, ages four to thirteen," continues Moritz, who like her colleagues is a native South Dakotan.

The Orion Classic, initiated in 1996, is their golf fundraiser. The event is the brainchild of Mark Amundson, himself a former South Dakota Amateur Golf Champion. By profession, Mark was a physical therapist for the PGA Champions Tour. It was during this time that Mark became acquainted with many of the Senior Tour players, particularly Graham Marsh, who counts the 1997 U.S. Senior Open among his seventy worldwide wins. As Mark developed his idea for a charity golf event for Children's Home Society, Marsh partnered with him and became instrumental in recruiting more than forty Champions Tour players to appear over the twenty-year run of the Orion Classic, including the likes of Dave Stockton, Hale Irwin, Bruce Fleisher, Morris Hatalsky, Butch Baird, and Jim Thorpe.

A generation later, many of the current professionals are recruited by native South Dakotans and PGA Tour winners Tom and Curt Byrum. The brothers were raised in a wide spot in the road called

Onida, populated by less than seven hundred souls in total, located in the geographic center of the state.

"Orion Food Systems has been our title sponsor from the beginning and their numerous vendors have been very supportive of our event," adds Moritz, who coordinated the first fourteen tournaments. "We have welcomed teams from Minnesota, Nebraska and Iowa in addition to those from South Dakota." Orion Food Systems sets the bar high through their title sponsorship gift along with additional donations, and many of their staff are among the event's volunteers.

There's no "Dakota discount" to play in this marquee event—corporate foursomes are $6,000, which also includes the pre-tournament Sunday evening dinner program, where the organization's vast mission is showcased. "Those of us who hail from the upper Midwest are very proud of our roots, loyal to the area, and realize this organization does great work," states Weber. "Not only do they pay a premium for our event, but many teams come back repeatedly, and continue to support us year after year." Overall the golf event has added more than five million dollars to Children's Home Society's coffers, and in recent years, the annual net approaches a half-million dollars.

Some of the funds raised by their golf event are helping fund a prevention initiative with a goal to reduce domestic violence and child abuse. "It's our hope that these proactive programs might someday put us out of business entirely," concludes Tom Roberts, jokingly.

Until that unlikely day arrives, it's good to know that Children's Home Society of South Dakota will continue to make their most vulnerable citizenry safe, just as they've been doing for more than 120 years.

For more information visit: www.chssd.org

Chip In for Carly's Club

Tragedy. Compounded by tragedy. Followed by the ultimate tragedy. But for all this heartache and loss, reminding one of the fragility of human life, ultimately this story uplifts. It's about the buoyancy of a little girl's spirit and her desire to give back when so much was taken from her so soon. It's a story about a loving, altruistic pre-teen as cute, saucy and memorable as her name: Carly Collard.

When first-grader Carly first complained of a headache in 1999, her pediatrician wasn't nearly as concerned as her adoptive parents, Chuck and Carole Ann Collard. Call it a parent's intuition, or the fact that catastrophic misfortune can occasionally come in threes. "We insisted on a CAT scan, and I remember how the technician wouldn't look me in the eye when she came out of the x-ray room," sighs Chuck Collard, recounting a tale of adversity that strains the imagination. "It turned out to be a tumor at the base of her skull."

Carly was barely a toddler when her dad Tony, a non-smoker and dedicated triathlete, was diagnosed with lung cancer. "He was at my house doing some yard work with me on a Wednesday," continues Collard, incredulously. "He had a lingering cough, went to the doctor the next day. He was gone by Monday, less than a week later."

A few years later, Carly's mother Judie, who was Carole Ann Collard's age-contemporary aunt, started acting strangely. She became unusually nervous, shaky, unsteady, and quick-tempered. "We thought it might have been a delayed response to Tony's death. Turns out it was an inoperable brain tumor," states Collard, shaking his head. The very morning Judie shared her awful news, the Collard family was scheduled to meet a realtor for a likely relocation to New York's Westchester County. Instead of driving some six hours south of their Buffalo home, they rushed to Judie's house, just five minutes away. They took Carly with them when they left, ostensibly for the weekend. But the five-year-old never really lived with her mother again. She was enveloped in the Collard's embrace and was welcomed into their growing young family; soon she was flourishing at school, with her friends, and with various extra-curricular activities.

Judie's prognosis was less than six months. Though she ultimately survived two years with her tumor, she made the brutally difficult decision not to let her vivacious kindergartner see her in decline. "Carly really didn't see her mom the last year she lived," recalls Collard. "She had taken experimental drugs to prolong her life, and they ravaged her physically. It must have killed her to do so, but she didn't want to scar, shock or emotionally damage her daughter. She didn't want to be remembered in this diminished state. We though it truly courageous."

After the funeral, Carly asked matter-of-factly how old her dad had been when he died. Told age thirty-nine, she asked the same question about her mom. Also thirty-nine. "But I quickly reassured her that most people lived until their 70s or 80s, like her grandparents," recalls Collard. "Obviously we had no inkling what was around the corner."

After the brain tumor diagnosis, which occurred just ten months after her mother's passing, Carly took up residence at both the Women & Children's Hospital of Buffalo and Roswell Park Cancer Institute. "That first surgery was nine hours," recalls Collard. "I remember feeling so envious of the parents who were just there for tonsillectomies and ear tubes."

Because she had been inundated with gifts, toys and balloons from her large Italian family, Carly would walk the halls dispensing her bounty to other children who had fewer playthings or distractions. The Collards had also received some monetary donations, totaling a couple thousand dollars. "I asked Carly what we should do with the money, what charity we should give it to," as he recalls with wavering voice an indelible conversation more than fifteen years past. "She said, 'let's start our own charity to help kids.' I said 'what will we call it?' She looked me in the eye for what seemed like ten seconds, and then responded emphatically, 'Carly's Club.'"

From this humble beginning, Carly's Club has now raised over three million dollars for pediatric patients and their families. This money has gone towards family counseling, therapeutic play programs, caregiver support programs, a variety of special events at Halloween and Christmas, and picnics and tailgates with the hometown Bills and Sabres.

"The 'aha' moment for us came when a hospital administrator handed us a pamphlet with general guidelines about our hospital stay," states Chuck Collard. "We innately understood that it wasn't a pamphlet that was needed, but a total process. We decided to focus our efforts on helping families with diversionary activities for healthy siblings, better care for the ill child, additional research, and anything we could do to make this emotionally catastrophic journey easier for both the patient and all of their loved ones."

Carly lived for more than three years after the diagnosis. Many good times ensued, as well as many challenging ones; she endured just one additional surgery but also three relapses and more than three hundred days hospitalized. She spent five months in Boston, where her "brother-cousin" Matthew attended first grade, and baby "brother-cousin" Josh spent his infancy in the local Ronald Mc-Donald House. After one powerful round of experimental drugs that actually slowed down the tumor's growth, her liver shut down. She was still shy of her twelfth birthday when she passed in 2002. "It amazes us to think that ninety-five percent of those we are helping today never met Carly," concludes her adoptive father. "But thanks to all the great work done at the Roswell Park Cancer Institute, where Carly's Club is located, her spirit and life force live on."

Stuart Scheff is a family friend of Chuck and Carole Ann. It was his idea back in 2005 to turn what had been a traditional, full-field charity golf event into a hundred-hole, one-day marathon that was coined Chip in for Carly's Club. Scheff raised about seventeen thousand dollars on his first try, and invited other golf nuts from his social circle to test their own endurance the following year. Players solicit per-hole pledges from family, friends, and colleagues, and over the years nearly one hundred different golfers have taken part.

Through this highly unusual golf event alone, nearly a million dollars has been raised for Carly's Club. It's a festive, high-spirited day, matching perfectly the effervescence of the darling young girl whose memory it honors.

For more information visit:
www.chipinforcarlysclub.org

The CJR Invitational

Memorial Foundation

In Loving Memory of Caleb Joseph Regenski

When a child dies in a sudden accident, shock and numbness are a parent's precursor to grief. When a child suffers a long, slow demise from a terminal condition, parents can attempt to steel themselves for the inevitable, unthinkable as it seems. Pennsylvanian Joe Regenski was caught in the in-between. When the light of his life, his firstborn child Caleb, took violently ill with flu-like symptoms, it was unfathomable to think the toddler would be gone in little more than a week. His father continues to process the heartache, still trying to make sense of it all, years later.

"He was a happy, rambunctious little boy," recalls Joe. "He was an only child, and could really entertain himself. He loved his Tonka toys, hearing country music, he was fixated by the Pixar movie Cars, he watched it constantly," relates his restaurateur father.

With the reassurance of their family practitioner, at first Joe and his then-wife Nichole thought their boy had a terrible bug. But within a day or two, unable to keep either solids or liquids down, Caleb stiffened up in their arms, became unresponsive. His eyes rolled backwards. His parents were soon to learn that their baby was suffering a series of strokes.

Another doctor suggested it might be meningitis, but as the symptoms continued, a CAT scan revealed medullablastoma-a brain tumor. A life-flight helicopter was made ready to take Caleb to the Children's Hospital of Philadelphia, but not before he was intubated. "The drive to the hospital was the longest two hours of my life," recalls Joe, who just days later made an even tougher drive, back to his northeastern

Pennsylvania home to begin making funeral arrangements.

The first big shock Joe dealt with in Philadelphia was the sight of that small body wired up to massive machinery, tubes everywhere, completely immobilized. As he began to get his bearings, he

hometown of Hawley, in the Poconos, not far from Scranton. It was my family, Nichole's family, those still living in the area, and those who flew in from other parts of the country."

After the emergency surgery to remove the tumor, a matter-of-fact surgeon deliv-

soon realized that most of the other kids on the PICU (pediatric intensive care unit) ward didn't have anyone with them. "There were nearly two dozen of us who descended on the hospital," relates Caleb's dad. "We are many generations deep up at Lake Wallenpaupack, near my

ered the crushing news. In his medical opinion, it was malignant, had spread, and that the Caleb they knew and loved was no longer. "He more than likely would have been in a vegetative state for as long as he lived," sighs his dad. "Because the threat of cancer had spread, the only organ we could donate were his corneas. It gave us comfort to know that another child would be able to see the world thanks to Caleb's eyes. We also donated his brain for further study, in the hopes we could assist other families. We made these decisions prior to taking him off of life support."

Few marriages can endure the strain of losing a child, and Joe and Nichole divorced soon after Caleb's passing. Wanting to honor the memory of his lost son, Joe decided to create the CJR Memorial Foundation.

"Joe and Nichole were very fortunate to have so much family support at the hospital," offers his wife Randi, a rekindled love from many years prior, before they married others and began their own families. "But so many kids are left alone," adds Joe. "Their parents have to prioritize their lives. Of course they are dedicated to their sick child. But they also need to pay the rent, put food on the table, provide for the kids who are still at home. That was the initial focus of the CJR Memorial Foundation. To provide monetary support for these distressed families, so they don't have to choose between being at their child's bedside, and earning a living to keep the family afloat. As our literature states, no parent should ever have to prioritize a payment or job before the care of their sick child."

The first fundraiser in Caleb's honor was a basket raffle, organized by close family friends, which took place in the spring of 2007, just months after his passing. Eventually Joe initiated a memorial golf tournament, named the CJR Invitational, which quickly gained a foothold in the community. As the fundraising ramped up, it allowed Joe and Randi to begin funneling monies towards other worthwhile causes.

Their second initiative was to fund a room at the original Ronald McDonald House, near the Children's Hospital of Philadelphia, with a plaque honoring Caleb. "Only one parent can stay in a child's hospital room overnight," adds Randi, whose own daughter Olivia spent time at the hospital some years after Caleb's passing. "It's a wonderful place, a home away from home, for parents and families to stay at no cost, in some cases for up to a year, while their child is being treated."

A third aspect of the foundation's focus is brain cancer research at the hospital where Caleb was treated. While these three causes are ongoing, it is a one-time bequest that might be closest to Joe and Randi's heart.

In 2014, thanks in large part to the money raised annually at their golf event, and with help from a generous grant from the Pennsylvania Department of Community and Economic Development, their foundation helped fund the CJR Memorial Playground in Hawley. With room for up to 150 children of all ages, abilities and physical challenges, it is a tangible way for Joe and Randi to stay connected to Caleb. It is lost on no one that upon the playground's unveiling, Caleb would have been the ideal user, full of life at nine years old, running from station to station, jumping, swinging, perhaps hanging upside down.

Adds Randi, "this area of northeast Pennsylvania has huge economic challenges. We are gratified we can offer the many families struggling financially a healthy, no-cost alternative to bond, stay active, and enjoy each other's company."

"Writing checks to these causes we support is wonderful," concludes Joe. "But the playground we helped fund is something we can see, touch and visit. It somehow keeps me closer to my son's memory."

The brain tumor he suffered from was so ruthless that in less than a fortnight Caleb turned from an energetic toddler to an insentient being with no discernible brain activity. However, thanks to the dedication of Joe, Randi, and the ongoing support of the CJR Invitational by hundreds of sympathetic neighbors, customers and friends, Caleb's spirit continues to burn brightly. He was gone in just ten days. But the memory of his ebullience and his sense of wonder remains strong nearly ten years after his tragic passing.

For more information visit: www.cjrmemorialfund.org

Corvias Foundation

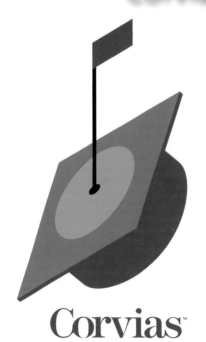

Corvias foundation

TEE UP FORE OUR FUTURE

Creating successful public-private partnerships is at the core of what Corvias Group does as a fully integrated development, construction, and property management firm. These partnerships build student housing, create solutions for storm water infrastructure challenges, and develop communities for the military. At the heart of this East Greenwich, Rhode Island-based company is serving military families.

Corvias Foundation, which is the charitable offshoot of the privately-held parent company, takes this support to an entirely different level. This altruistic entity provides much more than just shelter for our military families scattered about the nation.

The Latin translation of the word Corvias (pronounced similarly to Orpheus) is as good a description of the foundation's mission as anything else: "by the way of the heart." The mission statement for the foundation, which commenced operations in 2006, is "Imagine, Empower, Reach Higher." At the center of their philanthropic activities is helping active-duty military family members reach their educational goals.

To that end, their annual golf event, called Tee Up Fore Our Future, helps fund nearly a dozen individual fifty thousand dollar scholarships for the children of active military personnel every year. In addition, the foundation offers twenty separate five thousand dollar grants, which are used primarily by the spouses of active duty personnel. "The scholarships allow these young students to reach higher, and consider colleges and universities that, without our financial assistance, would be unaffordable," explains executive director Maria Montalvo. "The grants are more flexible, which is exactly how these military families have to live their lives, as they are so often in motion. This grant money can be used for childcare in a new city, to obtain certifications that have lapsed, keeping professional credentials up-to-date, to pick up additional college credits

when courses had to be abandoned in mid-semester because of a base reassignment or other relocation. Anything that makes an often challenging lifestyle a bit easier."

The vast majority of charity golf events, no matter how prestigious, elite or star-laden, generally take place in the same city year after year, if not the same golf venue. However the Corvias Foundation's is peripatetic in nature, and since its 2008 debut has taken place at some of the nation's most exclusive golf venues, geography be damned. The attendees, much like the mili-

tary families they are supporting, live all over the map. So they have visited Merion outside Philadelphia, East Lake in Atlanta, and Pinehurst in North Carolina. Put another way, many standard-issue charity events are held at a country club. But it's only the most rarified that, among other far-flung locales, pay a visit to The Country Club, outside Boston.

Over time more than three hundred military families have been assisted by Corvias Foundation, which has some seventy different companies donating to the

cause. "We try and keep everyone in contact as best we can, like a family, so our donors and beneficiaries can keep up with each other. It's not a 'one off' donation, but more of an ongoing relationship," explains Montalvo.

John Picerne is the founder and CEO of the billion-dollar company, which has over one thousand employees. In addition to supporting numerous other causes, the philanthropist personally contributes a seven-figure donation to the foundation each year. "It's not up to us to tell our beneficiaries what they need," explains the native Rhode Islander. "We're listeners. They tell us what they need, and we attempt to provide the financial wherewithal for them to achieve their goals. Hopefully as they reach their goals and become successful, they will reach back, help others, and continue the same philosophy. We consider our golf tournament unique because it honors military families but also because it's played at once-in-a-lifetime courses."

Unlike many charitable entities that derive the bulk of their annual donations from a golf event, the Tee Up Fore Our Future event is just a small piece of the foundation's overall philanthropic puzzle, approximately ten percent. "The fund raising element of our golf event is important, but we also strive to inform, entertain and enlighten our important partners, who hail from at least twenty different states. Whether they have business relationships with us or are mentoring our scholars, we strive to let them really understand how their generosity helps these military families in need," states Montalvo.

"It's important we show our partners an exceptional time, because in addition to pledging four- and five-figure donations to the cause, they are also flying at their own expense into whatever city we are hosting the event, and picking up their own transportation and lodging costs. Needless to say, with these types of committed individuals on our side we pull out all the stops to insure they have a meaningful and unforgettable experience with us."

Speaking of the marquee venues where the foundation holds its annual golf soirees, Montalvo concludes, "One of the things we like to do for our supporters is open doors they might not be able to open for themselves."

Sounds exactly like what Corvias Foundation does for its worthy beneficiaries.

For more information visit: www.corviasfoundation.org

The Cragmont Golf Tournament

Many tournament logos have deep meaning, but upon close inspection, The Cragmont's is particularly significant. "The modern cross represents God's grace reaching up to heaven and down to earth providing a bridge across a great chasm. Additionally, it reaches out to cover all mankind," begins tournament founder Rick Watson. "The circle represents God as the Alpha and the Omega, the beginning and the end. At the root of our purpose lies the passion to minister to our fellow man in a manner that pleases Him."

The mountains and resulting valley represent the geographical position of Cragmont Assembly, the tournament's beneficiary, lying in the Swannanoa Valley on Mount Allen, near Black Mountain in the western reaches of North Carolina. The valley further represents the host course for the tournament since inception, Happy Valley Country Club, in Wilson, fondly referred to as "The Valley."

Watson initiated the event in 1980 to benefit the mountain retreat for the Christian denomination known as the Original Free Will Baptists, or OFWB. The OFWB consists of approximately thirty thousand members and 240 churches that are primarily located in eastern North Carolina. In 1945 the OFWB purchased 118 pristine, wooded acres on Mount Allen near Black Mountain, for the purpose of enriching the ministry. In the late 1970s the main housing structure on the campus, part of the original purchase, had fallen into disrepair. It was razed and a new structure was built to accommodate visitors. But the cash flow needed to run the operation was impeded by the debt service necessitated by the new building.

Watson is now retired from a lengthy career in banking and finance, but has clear memories of the heady interest rates that were prevalent thirty-five years ago. "If you owed money, it was a daunting task to pay the interest on any loan. The golf tournament was initiated to help with the

debt service. I think the profits that first year may have paid a week's interest on our loan. But it was a start."

The Cragmont quickly gained popularity and by 1990 required two days to host three hundred golfers for a single round of captain's choice golf. The participation grew to four hundred, and by the end of the 1990s nearly five hundred players over three days. A fifteen-year period averaged 354 golfers annually. "Some of our regulars are avid church-goers, who rarely pick up a club all year long except at our tournament. Others are avid golfers first and foremost, but the common denominator among all who participate is a caring spirit that exists among these individuals of varied lifestyles and handicaps."

Since the tournament began, Cragmont Assembly has grown from a few weeks of summer camping into a year round camping, conference and retreat center, annually serving over two thousand campers, families and church groups. They make use of the forested acreage for reasons that might be spiritual, religious or personal in nature. The half dozen lodges on property can accommodate 240 visitors, who enjoy recreation spaces, full dining facilities, and such amidst the beauteous grandeur of the Blue Ridge Mountains. States Watson, "All who ascend the mountain to testify to a special presence of the Holy Spirit that touches each individual heart. This has truly become a special place." Their mission statement sums it up:

To operate, maintain and expand a conference center and place of retreat for all Original Free Will Baptists and seekers after Christ, who will come to Cragmont to experience inspiration, receive instruction and participate in recreation directed toward spiritual growth.

Charity golf tournaments, like virtually every other enterprise in the country, took a tremendous hit with the financial crisis of 2008 and 2009. "We had no strategy to combat the widespread economic woes so we took a look at what was most important to us, serving our fellow man in a manner that pleases God," continues Watson. "To accomplish that purpose we included the following statement in our promotional literature."

Please do not allow a negative financial situation keep you from playing in The Cragmont. Any arrangement you wish to make with the tournament director will be kept confidential. We want you to participate.

"That statement, which has become standard in our promotion, was accompanied by a twenty-five percent reduction in the entry fee and a substantial increase in our prize offerings. People understood what we were doing and why. That year we had just one person in the field who could not pay, but the astounding thing was that during this time of financial duress, at least half a dozen other participants paid an additional entry fee. Countless others made contributions of various amounts, all of which resulted in a minute reduction in profit. That is purely an example of good things happening when the spirit of man and the Spirit of God are in unison."

Looking back over thirty-five years of tournaments, Watson acknowledges that

initially, he never looked beyond the first event. I've come to understand that successful golf, and tournaments, and life itself, are built on faith and an ability to adapt. We have used proceeds at various times to pay debt, build facilities, and assist young people with funds to attend a week of camp. We believe all of those purposes have been blessed by God and we are grateful that we have had the faithful support of so many players, sponsors, and volunteers for many years."

Untold thousands have enjoyed and been moved by the spirit of The Cragmont, known mostly in Tar Heel country, but regardless, one of the most inspirational and successful charity golf events in the nation.

For more information visit: www.cragmontgolf.org

The Daniel Murphy Scholarship Fund Golf Classic

For a sterling example from the Greatest Generation, look no further than Daniel Murphy of Chicago. An All-State schoolboy halfback, he was so determined to serve his nation in World War II that he lied about his age and served in both Okinawa and Iwo Jima. He then came back to high school where he picked up where he left off as one of the Midwest's finest running backs.

That talent earned Murphy a football scholarship to the University of Illinois, but unfortunately academic apathy quickly set in and he didn't even last a full semester. He then spent his working life as a foreman at a dairy facility and the owner of a liquor store, always regretting having squandered the chance for a first-class education. With that perspective, he and his wife Carole made certain their three sons had the educational opportunities that he himself had frittered away. If only he had lived to see the enormous impact that he had on so many other lives.

The Daniel Murphy Scholarship Fund was created by his sons, their families, and their dear friends to honor Daniel Murphy's life of hard work that created educational opportunities. More than twenty-five years later, DMSF, working closely with over eighty private schools in Chicago and around the country, has given away a stupendous $120,000,000 worth of secondary education. More than 2,100 deserving and highly motivated young students hailing from every zip code of Chicago have received top-notch high school educations at college preparatory private schools in Chicago and at boarding schools nationwide. The brainchild of Jim and Bob Murphy, to honor the great sacrifices their dad made to send them to Loyola Academy, the Murphy boys continue to 'pay it forward' with their leadership of DMSF.

"If I had gone to my local high school, like other kids in the neighborhood did, who knows? I might have been a screw-up," begins Jim Murphy, who became anything but. "Our dad wanted us to get a first-class education, and he scrimped so we could," continues his oldest son, who spent a quarter century on the Chicago Board Options Exchange, and is now the chairman of a diversified company that focuses on businesses that provide renewable and sustainable resources to the Midwest. Two highlights of these endeavors are the largest ethanol plant in Western Michigan and a food company that facilitates the sale of local food from Midwestern farms to Chicago on a wholesale and retail level.

"At Loyola I learned to study, learned what it took to succeed. I was surrounded by high achievers. I was also fortunate enough to be awarded a Chick Evans Scholarship due to academic performance, financial need and years of caddying, which paved the way for me to attend Marquette."

Speaking of his years caddying at famed Bob O'Link, one of Chicago's infamous male-only golf clubs, Murphy adds with a wink, "I learned at least as much there as I did in high school and college!"

He also learned from his dad's example. "Working hard, which he did, doesn't automatically lead to success. A quality education is paramount. It increases your knowledge and critical thinking skills, affects your outlook, opens doors, and helps you make connections. That's why we started DMSF the year after he passed away, to honor our dad's memory and propagate his desire for kids from disadvantaged backgrounds to get solid educations."

Thanks to the generous donors who support the Daniel Murphy Scholarship Fund, more than four hundred teenagers annually are awarded $15,000 in scholarships, which adds up to a $60,000 commitment for their high school years. A healthy percentage of the $4,500,000 dollars of funding each year comes from one of the most impressive one-day golf events in the Midwest. Most charity golf events choose between quality and quantity. The DMSF event features both, in abundance.

"We have up to 450 players on five of Chicago's best courses," continues Murphy. "These have included Conway Farms, Onwentsia, Knollwood, Shoreacres, Exmoor, Northmoor and others of the same caliber. Most players choose to walk, so we use three hundred caddies, one third of which are our own DMSF scholarship kids, who choose to caddy in the summer and work towards becoming Evans Scholars, as I was. Everyone plays their own golf ball, so it's not the typical scramble

format. Afterwards everyone gathers under a huge tent at one of the host clubs, where we have a magnificent dinner, entertainment, and both live and silent auctions."

It helps that many of the attendees, like the Murphy Brothers, veterans of LaSalle Street (Chicago's answer to Wall Street) have deep pockets that match their deep commitment to the cause. Suffice it to say that a Myrtle Beach golf weekend or a three-night stay in Orlando aren't usually found on the auction menu.

"We have benevolent guys paying way too much to go play elite golf courses they could access on their own with just a few phone calls. It's not uncommon for someone to pay five figures for a dream golf trip somewhere exotic, and then never use it. But it's all for a great cause, so nobody stresses," continues Jim Murphy. "Our golf outing is integral to our success, as we net nearly $1,500,000 million for DMSF annually."

Apparently the golf gods concur. In the first twenty-six years of its existence, the Daniel Murphy Scholarship Fund Golf Classic has been blessed with lovely weather twenty-five times. No small feat in Chicago.

The founder marvels at how far they've come. "In the beginning, we were two brothers in our thirties, early in our careers, who donated some money to a cause near and dear to our dad's heart. We had a few founding board members, also our age,

who threw in a little themselves. Now we are a public charity and have thousands of donors and volunteers."

"There are many worthwhile charity golf events in this town, including several that are featured in this very book," concludes Jim Murphy. "But if you know the lay of the land, you don't schedule your event for the first Monday in June. That's our day in the sun."

There are many days in the sun ahead, bright futures everywhere, for the thousands of DMSF Scholars roaming the landscape. As the fund continues to ex-pand, both in endowment and reputation, more and more college admissions officers give these special applicants their full attention. Ninety percent are getting significant assistance, if not full college scholarships. More employers are learning of their work ethic and steadfastness, and as they enter the work force and become successful in their own right, eventually more funding will flow towards the Daniel Murphy Scholarship Fund. Just like the Murphy Brothers honoring their dad a generation ago, these beneficiaries will be intent on paying it forward themselves.

For more information visit:
www.dmsf.org

The Douglas G. Louis Invitational

There are many stressful occupations in the world: astronaut, air-traffic controller, Navy SEAL, policeman, and being Justin Bieber's publicist, just to name a few.

Add to that list the professional club manager, particularly in a high-end golf and country club environment, specifically around the New York metropolitan area, with a wealthy and hard-to-please clientele.

Randy Ruder is the general manager of Beach Point Club in the Westchester County town of Mamaroneck. He has been at the beach, yacht and tennis club for nearly a quarter of a century, tasked with serving his 650 members. "The club life is very intense," offers Ruder. "It's a seven day, morning and night commitment. We run the club from a business and financial perspective by day, and often need to shake hands and socialize with the members by night. It's a never-ending cycle."

Don Mollitor has more than thirty years of experience in the field, and is currently at the Seawane Club in Hewlett Harbor, Long Island. "Many of our 325 members send their kids away to summer camp for eight weeks. Then it seems the parents become the campers at our club, and our staff becomes the counselors!" He continues on a more serious note. "The stress is ongoing, and the demands are tremendous. We are working for affluent, challenging people, who want things done right. They travel in a first class manner, live in beautiful homes, and they want their club to be a home away from home."

Debbie Van Cura works closely with both men, despite the fact her day-to-day challenges

concern the polar opposite of the country club elite. She is the community coordinator of the AABR. Founded in 1956 in Jamaica, Queens, in those less politically correct times the acronym stood for the Association for the Advancement of Blind and Retarded.

The organization was founded by a small group of parents who were dealing with the tremendous challenges and heartache stemming from their children who were both blind and developmentally disabled. At that time, people with special needs were hidden away in institutions and defined more by their disabilities than abilities. The founders of AABR wanted more for their children-schools, services, a life of opportunities and choices. "There were no programs at that time for kids who were dually diagnosed. Over the years we have grown to the point where we are now serving more than a thousand individuals in every borough of the city," begins Van Cura, who has nearly forty years of tenure with the AABR.

AABR has twenty-five group homes, two separate day programs, a school for kids with autism, and a newer program for graduates who have aged out of the school. There is a family service unit that helps with medical support and respite care. There is also a drop-in center as well as a vacation home on the North Fork of Long Island that is available to clients and their families. With an annual operating budget of $36,000,000, government support provides basic funding, but the MCMA, which is the Metropolitan Club Managers Association, has been a major contributor since the early 1970s.

Over the decades the AABR has served several generations, many of whom stay in the program from childhood through adulthood. "We would not be where we are today without the support of the MCMA," continues Van Cura. "They are phenomenal. They have allowed us to open additional homes, expand our programs, retrofit houses to accommodate our special needs clientele, and basically pick up the slack when the government funding runs its course. Our partnership has been essential in allowing our agency to develop to the degree it has. We have houses that have been named after certain club managers and one home that is even

called the MCMA home."

Referring to his organization's ongoing commitment, Don Mollitor adds, "We realize we live in the real world, even though we don't necessarily work in the real world," referencing both the harsh reality of the special needs individuals served by AABR and the rarified country club life.

"The club managers become involved in the lives of our people," continues Van Cura, explaining the enduring support. "It's not just about giving money or raising funds for the organization. They get to know and care about them. Many of them will buy holiday gifts for those they've become attached to. It becomes a personal interest, and not just a charitable deed."

Both Ruder and Mollitor's longtime involvement goes beyond their affinity for those being helped. It extends to those doing the helping. "People like Debbie, Audrey Sachs, Frances Stillman, Chris Weldon, Tom McAlvanah and many of the other executives and volunteers at AABR have become friends and close acquaintances over the years," states Mollitor, a former tournament chairman. "My support of the organization stems in part because of the relationships I've developed among the staff. We as club managers think we have it tough sometimes, but these people are truly doing God's work. That's why I've been involved for twenty-five years."

"When you're asked to serve on the tournament committee initially, many of us do so out of obligation, just another task that needs to be addressed," offers Ruder, thoughtfully. "But over time you begin to develop a true interest and an emotional connection to the organization and the people they serve. In my opinion, that's why the bond has been so strong for so many years. At first you do it because you have to. Eventually you do it because you want to."

The golf tournament, now more than forty years old and perpetually attracting upwards of two hundred participants, is named for Douglas Louis. He was the general manager at Long Island's Muttontown Club, and was an ardent supporter of the cause in the early 1970s. "It was a real marriage right from the start," offers Van Cura. "AABR was looking for a benefactor to help raise funds, and the MCMA's newly formed charity committee was looking for an organization to support."

Support has come to the tune of six and a half million dollars over the years. The astonishing success is partially due to the local geography. Metropolitan New York is the nation's single greatest golf area, with a surfeit of world class courses. The tournament has been at Westchester Country Club for many years, but has also visited Winged Foot, Quaker Ridge, Century Club, Brae Burn, Old Westbury, Glen Oaks, and many highly desirable venues. In addition, the ancillary fundraisers such as the robust ad journal that's produced and the numerous raffle chances sold all add greatly to the bottom line.

"We have the perfect storm to run a successful event," concludes Mollitor. "First off it's our job to know how to run golf outings, we do so on a regular basis. Our individual club members will support the event because they're philanthropic in their own right, and as avid golfers they get excited about playing great courses. We also solicit meaningful support from our many vendors. We're truly in the sweet spot."

The AABR and the MCMA. To the wider world, just a series of disjointed letters, a bowl of alphabet soup. But considering the disparity between their respective missions, the synergy between the organizations is amazing. The club managers are tasked with

keeping the powerful and privileged happy and content. Those working for the nonprofit are trying to help those who've been dealt a rough hand lead meaningful and dignified lives. This long-time partnership is a fruitful union, bettering and enhancing both organizations. For those involved and in the know, the letters match perfectly.

For more information visit: www.aabr.org

The East Lake Invitational

It is no surprise the East Lake Invitational is such a rousing success, just a few years old but generating significant six figure donations annually since its 2011 inception. In a way it mirrors its beneficiary, the East Lake Foundation, which has also thrived. Though for the foundation, it's been a longer, slower road.

In the early 1990s Atlanta developer Tom Cousins was moved to action by a newspaper article stating that a disproportionate number of prison inmates in New York State hailed from just a couple of zip codes. In essence, crime breeds crime, and certain low-income neighborhoods were extremely fertile in producing career criminals. The East Lake Meadows public housing development in southeast Atlanta, with its dilapidated housing stock, violent streets and sub-standard schools definitely fit the bill.

Cousins had recently purchased the famed East Lake Golf Club, historically significant as the boyhood playground of legendary golfer Bobby Jones. But that romantic pedigree was completely obscured by the demise of the club and the disastrous, high-crime neighborhood in which it sat. "The club was dilapidated, insolvent and on the auction block," begins the club's chief operating officer Chad Parker, who came aboard in 1996. Cousins bought the club for four and a half million dollars in 1993, and at great risk considering its geographical undesirability, poured $27,000,000 into its refurbishment.

Wooing corporations as members, Cousins found success by ensuring that all net proceeds from the club's operations would be funneled to the newly formed East Lake Foundation, tasked with making wholesale improvements to the surrounding neighborhood. The charitable appeal worked to perfection. Over time the club filled its membership roster, and far more importantly, helped facilitate a complete overhaul of the neighborhood.

A few snapshots-prior to the foundation's formation the area's crime rate was eighteen times the national average. Unemployment was at eighty-six percent, and only fifteen percent of third graders met or exceeded state standards in math. Less than one-third of high school students graduated. The local public school was rated one of the worst in all of Atlanta. Now violent crime is down ninety-five percent. Ninety-eight percent of grade school kids meet or exceed state math standards and high school graduation rates went from thirty percent to nearly ninety percent, with eight of ten kids going onto college. The local charter school, which opened in 2000, is now considered among the city's finest. But statistics alone cannot capture the area's renaissance. Seven lyrical words uttered by former East Lake Meadows residents' association president Eva Davis sums it up. "We tore down hell and built heaven."

Adds Chad Parker, "We've come so far it's almost hard to remember how bleak the situation was two decades ago. It's a bad memory that has receded over time."

How to explain the astonishing turnaround? It's not one single initiative, but a basketful. The 650 low-income housing units at East Lake Meadows (forty percent of which were uninhabitable) were demolished and replaced with The Villages of East Lake, 542 mixed-income apartments with fifty percent reserved for public housing residents. Enrichment programs were brought to the area's residents, including health, wellness and job training. A junior golf academy, which eventually became The First Tee of East Lake, opened in the

neighborhood, along with several other recreational options. Something as simple as opening an actual grocery store with fresh food made a profound difference, so residents didn't have to rely on convenience store options. "By showing people there is light at the end of the tunnel, giving them a fair shake in a variety of ways, they can thrive and succeed. We've proven it here," states Parker.

If imitation is the sincerest form of flattery, those closely associated with the foundation should be blushing. After being inundated with requests to share their "blueprint" for success, in 2009 the East Lake model was, for lack of a better word, franchised through an organization called Purpose Built Communities. Using the intellectual property established in the former wasteland that was East Lake, they have since begun to resurrect other areas

plagued with intergenerational poverty and little hope for the future. They work with many local organizations in high-risk neighborhoods in cities like Omaha, New Orleans, Houston, Charlotte, Indianapolis and Columbus, Ohio. They have all employed the Purpose Built Model, based on East Lake. And it doesn't hurt to have powerful advocates like Tom Cousins, Warren Buffet, and hedge fund king Julian Robertson as financial backers for Purpose Built Communities.

Three separate revenue streams add some two million dollars annually to the coffers of the East Lake Foundation. The first is the net proceeds from the golf club, after expenses. The second is provided by the PGA Tour, which contributes significantly to the cause because they hold their ultra-prestigious Tour Championship by Coca-Cola on the famed golf course every autumn. And the third are the proceeds from the East Lake Invitational. "Some years ago the PGA Tour eliminated the Tour Championship Pro-Am," explains Parker. "The dollars the amateurs paid to play with these elite tour pros were significant, so we saw an opportunity to create our own fundraising event."

Many high-profile charity golf events use either celebrities or tour pros as a draw. Employing the "belt and suspenders" approach, the East Lake Invitational does both. Besides a wide range of well-known personalities from the worlds of sports, stage and screen, there's also a smattering of tour pros at East Lake, there to offer a tip, play a hole, hit a tee shot, etc. Hosted by veteran pros and Atlanta residents Stewart Cink and Billy Andrade, there have been appearances by Matt Kuchar, Webb Simpson and Bill Haas, among others.

For those without the inclination or financial wherewithal to play the main event on Monday, with its five-figures-per-foursome price tag, there is a lower key and far less expensive event on Sunday. Instead of playing with high-wattage stars, the donors play with kids from the local First Tee organization, some of them residents of the Village of East Lake, the mixed- income housing complex that replaced East Lake Meadows. The pairings might not be as glitzy as Monday, but can be both rewarding and informative. The kids show off their on-course progress, while detailing their strides in important areas off course. Besides, the Sunday event affords entry to that evening's pairings party, when anything can happen.

"You never can tell what might transpire at the pairings party and auction," concludes Parker. "One year Branford Marsalis, still in his golf shoes from the practice round, did an impromptu jam with a hired musician. Another time Jeff Foxworthy jumped on stage, did twenty minutes of material, and then stayed to help conduct our live auction."

These two celebs may share A-list status and a love of the game, but they surely have disparate personas. One is an urbane jazzman, the other the nation's favorite redneck comedian. It's easy to see that when two individuals from opposite sides of the spectrum can see the logic in embracing and supporting the East Lake Foundation, many thousands of others will be equally enthused.

For more information visit: www.eastlakefoundation.org

Ernie Kaulbach Memorial Pro-Am

Southern Connecticut's Fairfield County is so affluent that its nickname is the Gold Coast. But the gritty, industrial city of Bridgeport, decades removed from its manufacturing heyday, is more like heavy metal.

Unlike its tony neighbors Fairfield, Westport, Darien and Greenwich, Bridgeport has been beset by recession, unemployment, and intermittent hard times since the 70s, when many manufacturing concerns abandoned the northeast and moved overseas. The city's largest employer is currently Bridgeport Hospital, with six hundred physicians and a total of 2,600 employees. So it's appropriate that one of their longest-running fundraising efforts was initiated back in 1980 by a big-hearted, shirt-off-his-back plumbing supply magnate named Ernie Kaulbach. Fairfield County is full of bluebloods, but the golf-loving Kaulbach was decidedly blue collar.

"He was shy, but very kind," explains Austin Felis, his longtime accountant and friend of more than forty years. "He would never make a speech, he always avoided the limelight, but insisted on donating locally. One example of his amazing generosity: he ate at the same diner every day, and was friendly with some of the other early-morning patrons. One laborer he was acquainted with was down in the dumps one day. Ernie asked why, and the fellow said his truck had died. Ernie took him to the local dealership and purchased him a new vehicle that morning. That's the kind of man he was. Very giving, but wanted no fanfare."

Kaulbach made his considerable fortune during Bridgeport's halcyon days in the middle decades of the previous century, and was a member of prestigious Brooklawn Country Club in Fairfield. He and some of his fellow members, and some other golf buddies who played at Mill River in nearby Stratford, decided to start a charity event benefitting the Rehabilitation Center of Fairfield County, across the street from Bridgeport Hospital. They directed their funds

towards several physical therapy programs including those for young children with developmental delays.

"Despite Ernie's popularity at his club, at first Brooklawn wasn't interested in hosting the event," explains Stephen Jakab, the president of the Bridgeport Hospital Foundation, the facility's fundraising arm. "Back in 1980, charity golf events weren't as common as they've become, and few elite clubs opened their doors to outside play, despite how worthy the cause might be." Undeterred, Kaulbach found a home at the public-access Tashua Knolls, in his hometown of Trumbull, where the event remained for twenty-five years. The landscape had changed by the time the tournament committee approached Brooklawn again for the silver anniversary event in 2005. With the golf economy changing, Brooklawn was now happy to play host to the event.

Originally known as the Michelob Classic, with significant funding provided by a committed local liquor distributor, the pro-am format that Kaulbach and his committee initiated was a rarity during that era and proved popular with the patrons. The local golf community was excited to play with area professionals, and the pros were thrilled to play for a significant purse, in excess of fifteen thousand dollars.

Ernie developed cancer in the mid 90s, and received attentive and compassionate care from the nursing staff at Bridgeport Hospital. After he passed in 1997, it was decided that the fundraising beneficiary of the golf event would be the Norma Pfriem Cancer Center, and specifically its oncology nursing staff. "The nurses are the heart and soul of the hospital," explains Jakab, a Fairfield native who took his current position in 2000. "They are in constant contact with the patient, their family,

and the doctors. Ernie's friends and family decided to reward the nurses by providing opportunities for their continuing education both locally and nationally, in addition to assisting our efforts to enhance the cancer center itself. With the proceeds of a recent tournament, we were able to purchase nearly two dozen brand-new hospital beds for our cancer facility," states Jakab.

Coca-Cola took over as the main sponsor in 1999 and for some fifteen years reinvigorated the event as the second generation of players began to fill both the playing roster and volunteering roles. "Ernie was gone, and his closest associates, like Ben Costello, a multiple club champion at Mill River, were edging towards retirement. The event needed fresh blood and renewed energy to maintain its preeminence in the area," offers Austin Felis, who serves as the sole trustee of the Ernest and Agnes Kaulbach Foundation.

Coca-Cola's involvement, from both a branding and financial perspective, has made what is now known as the Ernie Kaulbach Memorial Golf Classic more successful than ever, with net annual proceeds north of $150,000. "We now offer patients and their families a twenty-four-hour chaplaincy program," explains Jakab. "So we can provide spiritual care in addition to medical care."

Thirty-five years after its founding, now firmly ensconced at venerable Brooklawn, the tournament maintains momentum. "Every year we gather our volunteers, who are the linchpins of the event, for a presentation," explains Jakab, a former high school teacher. "Both the medical director and the nursing director of the oncology unit come to explain how the previous year's funds have benefitted the hospital. It keeps everyone motivated and excited about what we're doing."

"I'm sure Ernie would be thrilled to know that nearly two decades after his passing, the tournament continues to thrive and help those in need in this area," concludes Felis, referring to more than two million dollars raised since inception. "He used to say to me, 'I made my money in Bridgeport, and I'll give it away in the same place.' I'm gratified we can follow that directive."

States Jakab, "many of our patients are uninsured or on Medicaid. We are thankful that monies raised at our long-running golf event help make what has always been a tough task just a little bit easier for those battling cancer."

Other than hearing "you've got the part," there are no words sweeter to an actor's ear than "callback." It means the possibility of success and that good things might be around the corner. Kaulbach is a homophone, and the ever-popular event that the namesake initiated back in 1980 is anticipated throughout the region every fall. Besides a fun day at a great golf course, it means good things are in the offing for Bridgeport Hospital.

**For more information
visit: http://foundation.bridgeporthospital.org**

Emmaus Community of Pittsburgh Golf Classic

According to the Bible, Jesus went undiscovered by his disciples as he encountered them on the road to Emmaus. But later, when invited to break bread with them, he was both recognized and venerated. "The moral of the story is that when you really look closely, and share your life with someone, you can see them for who they truly are. It's said that you can see the face of God in every individual you encounter, and learn that despite their challenges, everyone has gifts, and they are all worth sharing." So explains director of development Tiffany Merriman-Preston, who has been with the Emmaus Community of Pittsburgh in varying capacities since 2003.

This faith-based organization provides family-style, lifelong care at individual homes for adults with varying ranges of intellectual disabilities. It was founded in 1989 by area natives Lorraine and Ken Wagner, who had already raised four children including a daughter with intellectual disabilities. "They gave up their own careers, and became the live-in caregivers in the first home they opened, in 1994," states Merriman-Preston.

The Emmaus Community is based on the teachings of theologian, philosopher and humanitarian Jean Vanier, who founded L'Arche, a community in France for people with disabilities to actually live with those who cared for them. Explains Vanier, "the essence of our communities is this 'living with.' We are called, certainly, to serve with all our ability and to help those who are weaker to develop, but the foundation of this helping is found in friendship and the communion of hearts, which allows us all to grow."

In the first few years, prior to opening their first residential facility, the Wagners started a community center. The goal was to bring in families whose children had special needs or intellectual challenges, and figure out the best method to assist them. "The problem they were trying to solve was how to best care for those with intellectual and other developmental disabilities when their parents or family members could no longer do so."

More than sixty staff members, both full and part time, help support several dozen residents who live in nearly ten separate houses. The typical makeup of a home is three residents living with around-the-clock caregivers. Depending on their unique circumstances and their specific family situations, individuals arrive to become part of the community anywhere from their early twenties to early sixties. Just as widespread as their ages is the spectrum of intellectual challenges present. Some residents have apparent disabil-

ities while those of others are less visible.

In addition to running these various homes, the Emmaus Community also has a non-residential program, which has served untold hundreds of individuals since inception. This is where those in need who might still be living with their families receive life skills training, support, and guidance. Oftentimes those who take part in the non-residential program eventually transition into full time residency, based on space availability.

Therein lies one of the Emmaus Community's most daunting challenges—finding room and resources for the legions of people who need their assistance. They are only able to help a tiny fraction of those in or around Pittsburgh who would benefit from their ministrations. Government funding, mostly in the way of Medicaid waivers, foots part of the bill. However their annual golf event, now more than twenty years old, is an indispensible fundraiser and the single largest event on the calendar.

"We only can assist a few percent of those who would benefit from our philosophy, and live in our midst," continues Merriman-Preston. "We would love to have many more homes for residents, but the expense of purchasing and refurbishing these homes is daunting. That's why our golf event is so integral."

Over the decades the Emmaus Golf Classic has netted in excess of a million dollars for the Emmaus Community. Usually held at Nevillewood Country Club in Pittsburgh, on milestone anniversaries such as the tenth and twentieth it has been hosted by venerable Oakmont, the site of eight U.S. Opens. The corporate crowd lending their support is culled from the local legal, medical and business community, drawn not just to the high profile venue, but also to the importance of the cause.

"Regardless of one's strengths or weaknesses, everyone wants the same thing," adds Karen Jacobsen, the organization's executive director. "We all want to feel valued and respected. The Emmaus Community fosters deep, lifelong relationships between our residents, staff, volunteers, donors and the general public. We believe in the dignity of all people."

All the residents become productive members of society. Some are volunteers, others are paid employees, and still others are paid employees who are supervised. In addition to their work responsibilities, they all become part of the community at large. They take

classes, attend houses of worship, fulfill their civic duties, visit libraries, go shopping, and interweave themselves into the fabric of society.

Lifelong care means just that. Their original resident, a woman named Debbie, has been in the community since 1994. Her housemates came shortly thereafter, and they have been living together ever since.

Not only do residents of the Emmaus Community come to the golf event to meet the players at the pre-tournament breakfast and the concluding dinner, but several of them actually participate in the tournament. Marisa and Erin, who both became residents in 2014, are golfers themselves. They take their swings and fill out the scorecard alongside all of those who support the cause. It's a picture book example, illustrating that despite their intellectual challenges, those who live in the Emmaus Community are in their own way part of the mainstream, and attempting to do the same things in this life as anybody else.

For more information visit: www.emmauspgh.org

The First Tee of Central Ohio
Remembering Bob Morton

Though his formative years were in Tennessee, Bob Morton spent much of his life in Columbus, Ohio. It was in the heartland that his lifelong love of golf truly flourished, culminating with a wonderful honor bestowed by his many friends in the game.

The Morton Foundation was founded in 1998 by a prominent area businessman and Morton protégé named Tod Ortlip. The real estate developer gathered a group of like-minded business and community leaders who felt they, much like Ortlip, had benefited greatly from their own experiences in golf, and wanted to honor their close friend who had made golf a focal point of his own life. They had a desire to provide the same opportunity to kids in Central Ohio who might otherwise never be exposed to the game and the many life lessons it teaches.

"Golf was a huge catalyst to many of Bob Morton's successes," offers Rick Towle, an area golf professional and the executive director of the First Tee of Central Ohio. "He was a successful lawyer by profession. He played golf in high school, in college, he competed in many local and national amateur tournaments. He was a longtime official with the Columbus District Golf Association, and played the world over. He wanted to give others the same chance to do well with their lives, perhaps using golf as the mechanism."

The Morton Foundation might be the official name, but the hundreds of youngsters attending a golf-specific summer camp to learn the essence of the game were known simply as "Morty's Kids."

Beginning in 1999, young people between the ages of seven and fifteen were invited to a

once-a-week program that lasted throughout the summer at Walnut Hills Golf Course in Columbus. Equipment was made available, those who couldn't pay were welcomed regardless, and the instruction was provided by PGA and LPGA professionals from all over central Ohio. Morton himself, a low-handicap player even as a septuagenarian, took special pleasure in attending camp almost every week and helping the area youth begin to embrace the game he loved.

"I was the age of one of our typical golf campers when I first met Bob back in the 1950s," offers Tod Ortlip, smiling at the irony. "He and my dad were golf buddies, and when my father died young, Bob became like a second father to me." Ortlip found business success in many areas,

and never forgot the lifetime mentorship offered by "Morty."

"My company, Planned Communities, built The Lakes Golf and Country Club in 1989. I made Bob the first Chairman of the Board of Governors. He was the ultimate gentleman and young people used to say, 'when I grow up I want to be like Morty.' Because of the profound influence Bob had on my life I wanted to do something to honor him while he was still alive," continues Ortlip. "I wanted to create a foundation that would impact and possibly change the lives of kids less fortunate than their peers."

Towle, who began as a golf professional in central Ohio in 1994, came aboard the Morton Foundation in 2010. He was instrumental in transitioning the foundation into the folds of The First Tee, which first came to central Ohio in 2013. "Bob Morton lived a rich, full life. It was filled with family, friends, professional successes and an abiding affection towards the game he discovered in his boyhood. He was 94 when he passed away in 2005," continues Towle.

"It has been wonderful synergy. The goal of the Morton Foundation was to expose kids to golf, period, and we would subsidize any kid who couldn't afford it. But under the auspices of The First Tee, we have since expanded from summer camps to a year round program. The increased availability of the program is just one aspect of the change. In the bigger picture we now concentrate on exposing these kids to all the core values The First Tee teaches through golf. The game is the conduit to impart life lessons such as honesty, integrity, respect, sportsmanship, confidence, courtesy, and other vital attributes necessary to find success in the wider world."

The organization prides itself on the diversity of its clientele. Students are welcomed from the Buckeye Ranch, one of the state's leading providers of emotional, behavioral and mental health services for children, young adults and families. They partner with the Kipp School, and another group called Afternoon All-Stars, both of which are populated by youngsters from lower socioeconomic backgrounds. They invite kids from the Down's Syndrome Association of Central Ohio. The programming can be adapted and delivered using modified golf equipment when needed.

The First Tee of Central Ohio raises the bulk of the money needed for their programs through three distinct avenues. The non-playing outing is called the Memorial Tournament Luncheon, which takes place during the week of The Memorial, which is one of

the PGA Tour's most prestigious events. In addition to the official luncheon, the tournament provides passes and lunch for over one hundred local First Tee participants and chaperones. They enjoy an up-close view of the golfers, often get autographs, and the experience continues to sow the seeds for a junior golfer's continued affinity for the game.

On the course, there are two additional fundraisers. The First Tee of Central Ohio Golf Classic, and finally, the curiously named "Orty's Outing." Some think the name originated as a playful iteration of "Morty," others think it pays homage to Tod Ortlip. But the tournament brass says simply that they wanted to attract participants with a distinctive, easy-to-remember name.

The organization remains intent on continuing to teach the life skills and core values through the programming of The First Tee, as well as growing the game. Statistics have proven that overall performance in academic and social settings improves with exposure to golf. Four out of five participants in The First Tee feel greater confidence in their social skills with peers. Three quarters reported high confidence in their ability to do well academically. More than half of those queried felt like their meeting-and-greeting skills improved, and were better able to appreciate diversity in others.

The First Tee of Central Ohio is currently providing programming for about forty schools in the region. However, Towle, his staff, and sixteen dedicated board members are working to expand into every school in central Ohio.

Thanks to the continuing efforts of those who knew and admired Bob Morton, and the ongoing dedication of The First Tee, untold numbers of young people in and around Columbus are getting the chance to begin their own lifelong love affair with golf.

For more information visit: www.tftco.org

The Forsyth Country Club Celebrity Pro-Am

Having spent virtually all of his working life in the golf business, with nearly two decades of tenure in the PGA of America, John Faidley was embarrassed to admit that he really didn't know all that much about the First Tee of America.

"I honestly thought it was more of a 'golf first' organization," begins the longtime head professional of the prestigious Forsyth Country Club in Winston-Salem, North Carolina. "It wasn't until a chapter opened in our city in 2010, and after attending a few committee meetings, that I began to realize how many great values the program instills that go way beyond the game."

Using golf as a conduit, The First Tee teaches youngsters to embrace nine core values, including honesty, integrity, sportsmanship, respect, courtesy and perseverance. "When I heard some of those kids talk about how much the organization had done for them, how it helped them in school, and socially, I was so impressed," recounts Faidley. "Just the fact that they were so composed in a room full of adults in suits. I promise you, when I was their age I could never have stood up and spoken in a room like that!"

However, actions speak louder than words. The energized pro decided to ramp up what had been to that point a somewhat tepid fundraising effort in Winston-Salem. He began a celebrity-centric charity tournament to raise serious funds and greater awareness among his substantial membership for what had quickly become one of his favorite causes. It didn't hurt that Faidley was ensconced at one of the real bastions in this golf-mad state.

Forsyth Country Club, a Donald Ross gem with an avid membership one thousand strong, dates back more than a century. But in its long history, there had never been a celebrity event at the club, and the pro figured his members would really get enthused if one was created.

Bob Staak and Al Wood were instrumental in helping Faidley get the first event off the ground. Staak was a Division I basketball coach at Wake Forest and other marquee schools; Wood was a first-round NBA draft pick and was also Michael Jordan's roommate at UNC-Chapel Hill.

The regulars who have gotten into the habit of meeting and mingling with the attendees include your heavyweight champ, (James "Bonecrusher" Smith) your Heisman Trophy winner, (George Rogers) and your golf-loving rock and rollers (Edwin McCain, R.E.M.'s Mike Mills) And certainly there is a Tar Heel tinge to the proceedings, much to the delight of the Forsyth family, as the tournament field also includes UNC icons like basketball's Phil Ford and NFL great Lawrence Taylor. Wake Forest is well represented by NBA mega-star and native North Carolinian Chris Paul as well as the inimitable Muggsy Bogues, whose four-

teen-year NBA career was a startling achievement considering he stood just 5'3" tall. Former Duke and NC State athletes are also part of the action.

There is no shortage of Tar Heel-centric sports celebrities who would add additional "wow" factor to the Forsyth, which began in 2010. Several hall-of-fame college basketball coaches come to mind, not to mention the greatest hoopster who ever squeaked sneakers on a hardwood floor. But the tournament founder isn't sweating it. "I would love to get some very high profile attendees," admits Faidley. "However, given the choice between guys who can walk down a city street mostly unrecognized, and be truly friendly, approachable and charming, versus bigger name celebrities who might be less accessible to our membership, I'll take the former every time!"

Even though his event has been in existence for only a short time, this dedicated

pro has been so intent on building the impact of his local First Tee chapter that there is now a building named in his honor. The John Faidley Learning Center opened in 2015 at a nearby public golf facility in an area of town that was greatly underserved. "The most satisfying aspect of the center is the fact that, besides golf instruction, there's also a computer lab on the premises, so the kids can tackle schoolwork in addition to honing their golf skills. It's been very humbling, and I'm proud they chose to put my name on it, but equally proud we've been able to help thousands of kids since 2010."

The quick success at Forsyth has spawned additional fundraisers in the area, and in just a few short years the Winston-Salem First Tee chapter has gone from brand-new to one of the five biggest in the country.

"I feel our future looks bright because every year our returning celebrities get more comfortable with the event," explains Faidley, referring in this case to former and current NBA stars Gerald Henderson senior and junior. "When we asked Gerald senior to participate, he came down initially because he's a great guy. But he's obviously made some connections here, because he's been an enthusiastic participant ever since."

One of the reasons the Forsyth Event has been able to donate in excess of six figures every year of its existence is the fact that Faidley saves a pretty penny on airfare. "Most of our celebrity attendees live in North Carolina," states the thoughtful pro, a Virginian by birth. "They drive instead of fly. Some are natives, many are not, but they gravitated here for a variety of reasons when their careers wound down. They love the climate, culture, recreation opportunities, and everything that makes this state so wonderful. I guess in that respect they're a lot like me," he concludes with a laugh. "I wasn't born here, but I got here as fast as I could."

For more information email: johnfaidley@forsythcc.com

Fortune Marketing Unlimited, Inc.

FORTUNE MARKETING UNLIMITED, INC.

Golf and rodeo. As the English would say, they're as different as chalk and cheese. To many it would seem as ill-fated a partnership as any of Liz Taylor's or Zsa Zsa Gabor's sixteen combined marriages. However, for entrepreneur Loren Shapiro, an abbreviated stint marketing the Professional Rodeo Cowboy circuit was a steppingstone to a one-of-a-kind career conceiving, implementing and marketing charity golf tournaments nationwide. His company, Fortune Marketing Unlimited, has helped raise almost $200,000,000 for a wide range of charities over the last thirty years.

Shapiro comes by his business acumen and outside-the-box thinking naturally. His family consists of many successful entrepreneurs going back to the late 1800s. Back in the mid-1980s, it didn't take the recent college graduate long to realize that if IMG, his first employer, couldn't see the value in promoting charity golf events, he would go out and do it himself.

"I began at IMG on a Monday, and was off to my first rodeo in Reno that Thursday," reminisces the Massachusetts native, who also visited ports of call in Wyoming, Texas, Oklahoma, Washington, and Calgary during his brief foray into the big-belt-buckle crowd. "Among other things, I was there to make sure our corporate-rodeo sponsors were getting the exposure they were promised."

His axis tilted when he was invited to play in a charity golf event for underprivileged children put on by the rodeo cowboys at famed Colonial Country Club in Fort Worth, Texas. "I had never played in a charity event, or a scramble tournament," recounts Shapiro, who played soccer, basketball and golf at Tufts University outside of Boston. "Mainly because I was young and didn't have any money!"

His epiphany was that marketing a nationwide series of charity scrambles would be attractive to corporate sponsors coveting the affluent golf demographic. Working side by side with senior-level marketing executives from Fortune 500 companies that were also involved in the rodeo circuit, Shapiro learned they would theoretically support such an endeavor. The problem was that IMG had no interest. "They told me they didn't do charity. They couldn't wrap their head around the fact that corporations would be willing to pay to reach this affluent, philanthropic audience."

The distilled spirits company Seagram's bought into Shapiro's vision to the point that they not only signed up to be the title sponsor, but also paid IMG to buy out the non-compete clause he had signed as part of his employment contract directly out of college.

The Seagram's Scramble was supposed to debut in 1987, which was when Fortune Marketing Unlimited was formed.

After months of research and consideration, they decided to partner with the National Kidney Foundation as the benefiting charity. Ultimately, the nationwide program was named The Glenlivet Scotch Scramble, to better focus attention on the premium brand which was a new acquisition by the parent company.

In 1988, fifty tournaments were created from scratch, with all monies raised benefiting the National Kidney Foundation. Former football star and popular television broadcaster Pat Summerall was the first spokesperson for the tournament series. Other National Honorary Chairmen include Lee Trevino, Tom Watson, Fred Couples, Lanny Wadkins and current chairman Curtis Strange. The attending golfers were exposed to this little-known brand via tastings, and Seagram's benefited by their alliance with the health organization, which espoused a theory that drinking in moderation was beneficial to your health. In short, a win-win for all concerned.

One of the challenges was publicizing the events in states that forbade the advertising of distilled spirits. So in 1991, Cadillac took over as the title sponsor, with Seagram's taking a less prominent role. That partnership lasted nineteen years and ultimately grew to more than 130 events annually. After raising $120,000,000 for the charity since 1988, in 2006 Shapiro and his partner Skip Jenkins expanded the business beyond the National Kidney Foundation, increasing its reach to better serve major U.S. markets and to meet the desire of their primary sponsors. "We initially kept seventy-five NKF events, but added dozens more, including the United Way, multiple veterans charities, multiple cancer organizations, the Arthritis Foundation, Habitat for Humanity, and many hospitals including the Chinese Hospital of San Francisco and the Detroit Medical Center Foundation, among others. We grew from one charity to sixty-five and worked to expand and upgrade the selection of courses we offered, including venues such as The Olympic Club, Winged Foot, Oakland Hills, Oakmont, Pebble Beach, TPC Sawgrass and Pinehurst. We began raising even more money, and adding greatly to the bottom line of many charities, in some cases even tripling the amount of revenue they received prior to partnering with us."

Then disaster struck. The financial crisis of 2008 put General Motors into bankruptcy. Congress declared that any entity that received bailout money from the government was prohibited from spending on sports marketing or any other "frivolous" activity. States Shapiro, "What they didn't understand was that Cadillac was spending less than a million dollars for our program, but reaping more than forty million dollars in measured annual sales!" The program was such a successful marketing and sales tool that even without GM corporate sponsorship, the top fifty Cadillac dealers funded the program in 2009.

FMU understands that businesses may have philanthropic agendas, but primarily, their business objectives are driven by profits. In order to make sure that the program's sponsors continued to support the tournament for many years, FMU developed programs designed to generate sales. By offering attendees a dozen golf balls for taking a three-minute test drive at tournament venues, Cadillac showcased their new and improved product line to an audience who wouldn't otherwise consider the brand. The measured results: more than eight hundred new Cadillacs sold annually at an average sales price of fifty thousand dollars each. "We were capturing a new untapped audience who drove other brands and wouldn't ever have considered purchasing a Cadillac, which is what truly made the program a success."

Liberty Mutual Insurance saw the immense value of the program, took over the title sponsorship in 2010, and the relationship has been a runaway success from the get-go. They continue to renew their three-year contracts, Fortune Marketing Unlimited is doing nearly eighty events annually, and the program is netting in excess of seven million dollars a year for the charities.

"We have run more than 3,300 events since the company was founded," concludes Shapiro. "We've enjoyed success for a variety of reasons. We share our extensive tournament planning and management experience and provide a turnkey solution by providing all of the prizes, gifts, signage, management support, etc. This comprehensive package allows the tournament committee to focus on selling foursomes and sponsorships so they maximize proceeds."

"These tournaments provide great entertainment for important clients and prospective customers. People know that a Liberty Mutual Invitational event is first class, and will be a great day of golf for a wonderful cause. Liberty Mutual is dedicated to helping people lead safer, more secure lives. That is the objective of virtually all of our charities so their missions are exactly aligned. Also, while sponsoring a PGA Tour event offers a lot of glitz, it often requires that clients fly elsewhere to be entertained. Because the Invitational has so many events nationwide, Liberty Mutual can entertain clients in their hometown and help raise funds for a local charity in that client's community. The impact is enormous."

Just like the impact Fortune Marketing Unlimited has had on the charity golf landscape for thirty years and counting.

For more information visit: www.fortune-marketing.com
or: www.libertymutualinvitational.com

Friends of Callawassie Island

Friends of Callawassie Island, Inc.
FOCI
"Neighbors helping Neighbors"

If you're a golfer, you've doubtless heard of Hilton Head Island, one of the most beloved beach, bike and vacation destinations in the Southeast, featuring no less than thirty different golf courses.

If you love history, mystery, classic architecture, genteel Southern charm, nightlife, and fine dining, you're likely familiar with the sister cities of Charleston, South Carolina, and Savannah, Georgia, located just two hours apart.

However, despite its centralized location between these three must-visit destinations, which collectively draw some thirteen million tourists every year, probably not one in a thousand people has heard of Callawassie Island. It is little more than half an hour west of Hilton Head, perhaps ten minutes further from Savannah, due south, and an hour and change north to Charleston.

But forgive the full-time residents if they're not making daily or weekly pilgrimages to these ultra-popular vacation spots, because they have plenty to occupy themselves in their own piece of paradise. This nature lover's oasis is tucked serenely across a scenic causeway spanning Chechessee Creek, and is bordered by the Colleton and Okatie Rivers and Callawassie Creek. The community features eleven miles of coastline on 880 acres with properties on navigable deepwater, tidal creeks and salt marsh, and tranquil views of the twenty-seven-hole golf course.

Jeff Spencer, the club's general manager and director of golf, points out that legendary course architect Tom Fazio was able to design the trio of nine-hole tracks at a time when regulations still permitted a golf course to meander right along the edge of

the rivers and marshes. Therefore, the visual interest for golfers is natural, not manmade.

Giving to those in need is nearly as popular a pastime as golf for the residents at this little-known Lowcountry jewel. Elaine Diaz in the president of Friends of Callawassie Island, known as FOCI. This is an active and dedicated group of volunteers, devoting untold hours annually to better the lives and living situations of their neighbors in nearby towns through a variety of charitable giving.

"There are only about five hundred homes at Callawassie, and while it's an exaggeration to say that everyone knows everyone, it's not far from the truth. We have an intimate, caring community," begins Diaz. "Not only in terms of our fellow residents, but in our desire to help our neighbors in need. That is the essence of FOCI."

Like many charitable efforts that develop momentum over time, FOCI was initiated almost by happenstance. In 2000, Callawassie Island hosted a Carolina PGA pro-am golf tournament. That event generated an unexpected profit, so the organizers decided to give the surplus money to a local charity. Friends of Callawassie Island, Inc. was born.

Besides their annual autumn golf event called Tee it Up for a Worthy Cause, which provides the lion's share of FOCI's endowment, there are two other significant fundraisers. Closets, attics and garages are scoured clean every other spring for a gargantuan yard sale held at an area health center. On the yard sale's off year, the Callawassie Players take to the stage to perform an original musical play written and directed by Ms. Diaz. It is produced, staged, costumed and performed by island residents. All proceeds from the three performances are earmarked for FOCI.

"FOCI has become an integral part of life on this island, and it goes beyond the good feelings emanating from helping others," states Jeff Spencer. "Hundreds of residents volunteer at or participate in one or more of the fundraising vehicles, and about fifty thousand dollars is raised and given away annually. More than half a million dollars has been disseminated since inception in 2001. The success of these various events is a direct result of the tremendous support not just from island residents, but from the entire Callawassie staff, who are equally enthusiastic."

FOCI-supported charities provide direct assistance in the areas of youth education and recreation, health and human services, child care, children and women's shelters, programs for seniors, hunger, literacy, housing, and other expanded social services.

More than three hundred individual grants have been made to eighty different organizations, generally a few thousand dollars per grant. These organizations often run on a shoestring budget, and are very grateful for the assistance provided by FOCI.

One of the strange dichotomies in regards to the island's location is the fact that it practically straddles the county line between Beaufort and Jasper counties. The former is the wealthiest county in the state, while the latter is the poorest. The Boys and Girls Club of Jasper County is near and dear to FOCI, as it gets far less funding then the other area clubs on Hilton Head, Bluffton and Beaufort. Friends of Carolina Hospice, another favored charity, provides expert hospice care and services to all individuals regardless of their ability to pay. Heroes on Horseback provides safe and professional equine-assisted therapeutic activities for individuals in the Lowcountry with physical, intellectual or emotional disabilities.

Sometimes FOCI makes make one-off donations for a specific need. They recently provided funds to purchase team swimsuits for the local Carolina Hammerhead Sharks Special Olympics swim team. They were resigned to wearing

their individual swim attire as they headed to an important meet in Charleston, before FOCI intervened.

"Not everyone at Callawassie is retired, but it is a place where many individuals end up reinventing themselves in retirement," states Diaz. "We have numerous individuals who have been active in charitable work throughout their adult lives, but we also have others who came to embrace the concept once they moved here, had the time and the energy to devote themselves to these great causes, and meet scores of others who are likeminded."

"There are hundreds of wonderful communities nationwide where residents have literally dozens of recreational options," adds Gene Durick, a longtime FOCI board member. "But Friends of Callawassie Island is so entrenched, and so important to the lives of so many of our residents, it is considered one of our amenities along with golf, tennis, fishing, boating, fitness and the like."

With the majority of residents feeling fortunate to have found their way to this little-known island, it's no surprise so many embrace this altruism. It's more than a slogan. Callawassie is truly a small island with a big heart.

For more information visit: www.friendsofcallawassieisland.org

Genesis Golf Classic

A recent series of attention-getting cases has made the National Football League the reluctant poster child regarding the scourge of domestic violence. But even with its profile raised, very few people have any concept of how rampant this reprehensible behavior actually is. Consider this startling fact; one in four women will experience physical abuse in their lifetime. Let's make it even more personal. If a man has a mother, a wife, a sister and a daughter, statistics show that one of them will endure violence perpetrated by their male partner.

"When I first came to work here in 2011 even I was shocked to learn of the prevalence of violence directed towards women," begins Bianca Jackson, the Senior Director of Fund and Development at Genesis Women's Shelter in Dallas.

Like many shelters of this kind, to protect the residents the physical location of the facility is undisclosed. Suffice it to say it's located in a nondescript building in Dallas. The irony is that even though they only pay the city a dollar a year for rent, the work they do is priceless.

"There was a soup kitchen near here called the Stewpot," continues Jackson, recounting the 1985 origins of Genesis. "A priest named Jerry Hill noticed a woman who always stayed in her car with her kids after the meal."

When this woman was asked why, her response was both matter-of-fact and chilling. "It isn't safe for me to go home." Father Hill made inquiries, learning the nearest women's shelter was literally a thousand miles away, in Jacksonville, Florida. He approached the board of the nearby Austin Street Center for the Homeless, and shortly thereafter Genesis was founded. They grew from seven beds to fourteen separate rooms, and are now able to house up to forty women and children.

There is an on-site school to prepare the children of residents for a smooth transition back into their traditional school situation once their shelter stay has ended. The Simmons School at Genesis Women's Shelter & Support is a full-service, K-12 school with a full-time, certified teacher and an aide, and follows Texas curriculum in order to lead the students through their current grade level towards their reintegration into the mainstream.

Jackson has a healthcare background, and offers a medical analogy to explain the three arms of Genesis. "The shelter is like the emergency room at a hospital, and we limit stays to six weeks. Often this isn't long enough for a woman to revamp her whole living situation. Across the playground we have nineteen apartments, called Annie's House. Women can stay for up to a year with their kids. This is analogous to the hospital itself. Finally, we offer outreach counseling, where non-residents can get help from lawyers, counselors and social workers. This is akin to an outpatient clinic at a medical facility."

Genesis has one hundred full- and part-time employees, more than twenty of whom are counselors. They also have two thousand volunteers, who do everything from helping kids with homework, to putting on pancake breakfasts, to facilitating back-to-school fairs, to running their massive thrift shop, a major revenue source. Though the shelter assists up to 1,600 women a year their operating revenue comes solely from community support.

Community outreach is a vital component of the Genesis mission. "We speak at churches, fundraisers, Rotary Clubs, college

sororities," states Jackson. "Invariably a female audience member will approach one of us and confide that they've suffered domestic violence. You think you're speaking to 'them,' but the reality is you're speaking to 'us.'"

Speaking of their long-running golf event, CEO Jan Langbein offers, "Some of our regulars come out because we run a great tournament. But for many, this issue is personal. At Genesis Women's Shelter and Support we feel strongly that because men are fathers and sons and brothers that domestic violence impacts their lives because it impacts the women in their lives. Part of our field is comprised of men who love golf. Others are more connected to the cause, as they might have a mother, sister or wife who experienced domestic violence in the past."

"Our golf event is a way for men to take a stand against domestic violence, and for us to invite men to be part of the solution, to be the voice and hope for those who thought there was none," states Langbein, whose tenure dates back to 1991.

It would be easy to surmise that the majority of Genesis clients are part of the underclass or less educated, but that is simply not the case. "We assist many women who are put together, have great jobs, sit on boards, and maintain the appearance of propriety," continues Jackson. "But their secret ordeal is the volatile, unstable relationships they suffer with, situations that are unhealthy to begin with, and can easily deteriorate into outright danger."

Genesis has a yearly operating budget in excess of six million dollars. On the surface it might seem that their annual golf event, raising about $100,000, is little more than a trifle. But dollars aside, it is one of the most crucial fundraisers of the year, and has been for a quarter of a century.

"Our golf event is indispensible," concludes Jackson. "The fundraising is important, but its true value is raising awareness of this issue. This is because it is our chance to get about two hundred men together in a convivial atmosphere, and illustrate how important it is to curb domestic violence. Hopefully, at the end of every tournament, we have imprinted on two hundred men that abuse is never acceptable."

For more information visit: www.genesisshelter.org

George Archer
Memorial Foundation for Literacy

Long-time PGA Tour player George Archer seemingly had it all; he was tall, fit, and athletic, with a lovely wife and two attractive daughters. Originally hoping to last on tour for five years, he instead won more than forty professional tournaments across five decades. In addition to a dozen victories on the PGA Tour itself, he added the single most coveted wardrobe addition that every male golfer, amateur or pro, dreams of putting in their closet: a green jacket from Augusta National. Archer slipped one onto his broad shoulders after winning The Masters in 1969.

However, there was one thing the Californian didn't have, something startling in its simplicity and remarkable in its absence. Archer couldn't really read or write. Despite his fame, acclaim and position in the public eye, he was functionally illiterate.

Donna Garman was seventeen and George twenty-one when they met in 1960. "I was incredulous when he confessed he didn't have a driver's license," she begins, thinking back to that day long ago in his native San Francisco. "I asked why, he hesitated, then admitted he couldn't take the required written test because he couldn't read or write. I responded like any flip teenager would. 'Of course you can read and write!' But I was wrong."

From that day forward, Donna was his accomplice and confidant, devoted to a dual task: keeping his shameful secret hidden from the world, and working feverishly to help him overcome it. The former would prove much, much easier over time. They married in 1961, and up until Archer's death in 2005, after raising two daughters, Lynne and Elizabeth, and seeing them start their own families, which would

eventually include seven grandchildren, Donna worked on his literacy tirelessly.

Through decades of tortuous tutoring, flash cards and phonics work, mostly by sheer repetition, he struggled to perhaps a fourth grade level. But his writing was always by rote. Donna patiently taught him to write her name, the kids names, and phrases like 'Best Wishes' so he could sign autographs. Lynne, who became a special education teacher, tried to help him. But any name beyond one syllable, no matter how slowly the supplicant spelled it out, would throw him into a panic, and Archer would blank out. "He would ask for their business card, and tell them he'd mail them an autographed picture later," recalls Donna with a sigh. "I also taught him how to write 'I love you.' And I insisted he write it, all the time!"

It was this incredible love and devotion that sustained them as they tightly guarded this burdensome secret. Despite what he considered his 'mental block,' Archer wasn't stupid. He was a gregarious storyteller. He survived on the roads by knowing the shape and color of a stop or yield sign. He had great spatial awareness and a keen sense of direction. Without being able to actually read the name of a city on a map, he intuitively knew where he was in relation to where he came from. It was this innate ability that made him excellent at putting, a skill that would always be the strength of his golf game. He was eventually able to get a legitimate driver's license in the same manner that decades later he was able to finally get his 'Class A' card as a PGA professional. In both instances, the testing bodies administered oral, as opposed to written, examinations.

Despite his cleverness at hiding this crippling disability, Archer could have never pulled off this lifelong charade without help. Donna would fill out all customs declarations when they traveled overseas. Another key figure was Eugene Selvage, who Archer met as a teenager while caddying at the Peninsula Club in San Mateo, California. Selvage became a mentor, a friend and a sponsor. He owned a company called Lucky Lager beer, and sponsored the first professional event Archer won, the Lucky International, held at Harding Park in San Francisco.

"The generosity of Mr. Selvage allowed us to travel the tour in the early days, and we paid him back from George's winnings. But he never took anything above our expenses. He was a

man of character, and felt George was a kindred spirit," states Donna. Selvage also helped Archer by taking care of contracts, tax bills, and other documentation that he couldn't handle on his own.

In his teens George also caddied for Harvie Ward, the bon vivant amateur who captured both the U.S. and British Amateurs. Recalls Donna, "George admired his golf skill, but didn't think he treated his wife well, or worked hard enough on his game. He used to say to me 'he threw it away.' George was the opposite. He didn't have that type of talent, but he worked tirelessly to become as good a player as he could. His work ethic was amazing."

Despite his single-mindedness in the pursuit of great golf, he could never beat his 'mental block' with regards to reading. "He was fearful of humiliation his entire life," states Donna. "He was always the kid at the back of the class, told not to chime in, had to wear the dunce cap. He was kept back twice after second grade, then grew so tall they skipped him to fifth grade, without benefit of third or fourth grade. He was 'enabled,' which means ignored."

How Archer was granted a high school diploma remains a mystery. Perhaps in the mid-50s it was easier to slip through the cracks of the education system. He survived on a combination of wood shop, band, art class and a prominent position on the golf team. He took remedial classes, kept his mouth shut, got sympathy D's from the teachers, and was shuffled through the system. Donna Archer reports that the suburban San Francisco high school her husband graduated from came under harsh scrutiny years later for being a "diploma factory."

His wife reports that there were also hearing and comprehension problems. For the first decade they were together he called her "Donner" instead of Donna, and no matter how many times she told him the word was "idea," he would pronounce it "idear."

Archer felt embarrassment his entire life. He safeguarded this problem so closely in large part because he felt that if any golf competitor gave him grief and started to needle him about this profound disability, he would fall apart. His golf afforded him not only the ability to make a living, but a sense of confidence that was lacking in other areas.

It was for these reasons that after his death Donna and their daughters initiated the George Archer Memorial Foundation for Literacy. "I didn't want any child to have to suffer the way my husband did, and feel that type of intense shame their entire life."

The Foundation's mission is to fund and help train teachers, tutors and special education professionals to better identify children who are dealing with dyslexia and other disabilities. They provide books for local schools and libraries, with a special focus directed at kids who come from families with few if any books in the house, where reading isn't stressed, or with parents who aren't readers.

The George Archer Stroke of Genius Pro-Am Tournament has helped raise nearly half a million dollars for this cause. The event, approaching its tenth anniversary, is held at the Peninsula Club in San Mateo. The venue is symbolic, and brings Archer's story full circle. It's not just the fact it's where he first met Harvie Ward, or his great career mentor Eugene Selvage. Beyond that, the club saved his life.

"George told me when he was about eighteen he was in such despair he considered suicide," concludes Donna Archer, somberly. "He was distraught, and didn't want to end up as a bum in the San Francisco slums. This club literally turned his life around."

For those with profound reading disabilities, the George Archer Memorial Foundation for Literacy is also turning around lives, one child at a time.

For more information visit: www.georgearcherfoundation.org

The Healing Place Charity Championship

Tuscumbia, Alabama, in the state's remote northwest corner, is famous as the birthplace of Helen Keller. She lost both her sight and hearing as a baby, but overcame these drastic disabilities, which at that time seemed to be insurmountable. She eventually graduated from college and became a noted activist, speaker and author.

Closer to the Tennessee River in the neighboring city of Muscle Shoals, there is a unique treatment center called the Healing Place, the only facility of its kind in the state. Grieving, unmoored children receive the care and attention they need, much like Helen Keller did more than 135 years ago. Keller lost her main faculties, and Healing Place clients lost a loved one, usually a parent or sibling. But the commonality in both instances is that innocent lives descend into absolute turmoil through no fault of the child.

Kay Parker is the founder of the Healing Place. "Very simply, we are a center for grieving children. We provide support and counseling for children who've lost a loved one, most often a parent or sibling, due to accident, homicide, suicide or illness."

The facility was founded in 2002 by Parker, who worked as a grief counselor at a nearby cancer center. She realized that the needs of the region's youngest citizens were not being met adequately in regards to the grieving process.

The Healing Place's outreach program is a vital component of the operation.

"We fan out, and our handful of counselors visit forty-two schools in a three-county area," states Parker. "In the weeks and months following the death of a loved one, the surviving spouse is often overwhelmed with new and unfamiliar responsibilities. It is often difficult to bring the child to us, so we come to the child and visit the schools regularly. This takes the burden away from the remaining parent, who is often dealing with dozens of other issues and complications."

The center offers both individual and group counseling sessions, and often serves meals in the evening where families can bond together. "Nothing is homier and more comfortable than sharing a meal to-gether," continues Parker. "It offers a sense of comfort and normalcy to the kids and their families."

Group counseling is separated by the type of death of the child's loved one. Children who suffered the death of a loved one due to homicide or suicide have their own groups. In their grief support groups, children are surrounded by others who really 'get it,' and understand exactly what they are going through. They do not feel alone in dealing with their grief.

The Healing Place had a dozen clients the first year of operation. A decade later they were up to 350. Several years later the number crested 450. The death and accident rate in the region remain stable, but the Healing Place's reputation continues to grow, and more of the local citizenry seek out their services.

Thankfully the annual golf tournament that provides much of the center's funding also continues to grow. "I think about ninety percent of the center's annual revenues come from our tournament," begins Chad Parker, who ought to know. Chad's mom Kay is the founder, his sister Karen one of the counselors, and his childhood friend and longtime golf buddy Stewart Cink provides much of the PGA Tour star power that has made the golf event so successful since its 2003 debut.

"Supporting the Healing Place is a natural fit for me, and it's a pleasure to do so," begins Stewart Cink, who counts the 2009 British Open Championship among his half-dozen PGA Tour victories. "First off, it's in my hometown of Florence. Secondly, the entire Parker family are dear friends of mine; Chad and I even served as best man in each other's wedding. Thirdly and perhaps most importantly, my wife, Lisa, lost her dad when she was just eleven. It was a traumatizing event for her. Too bad there wasn't this type of counseling available for her as there is today, but it's gratifying to know we are raising funds for the Healing Place, and kids today get the help they need when a loved one is taken from them."

Cink recruits up to ten of his equally illustrious PGA Tour brethren, which is no easy conscription on a June Monday down in Florence, Alabama. The rest of the professional field consists of golf professionals (not the same thing as professional golfers) like Chad Parker himself. "It's a wonderful fit," explains Parker, "because the Tour pros are completely accessible to all the attendees, and meet and mingle throughout the day. But we have great pricing flexibility. The 'Eagle' teams play with a PGA Tour player, and these are mostly high-dollar corporate teams. The 'Birdie' teams play with a club pro, and are more affordable for individual players, or groups of buddies who want to support the cause in more modest fashion."

The traditional gift to all the pros every year might also be considered modest, but much anticipated nonetheless. Chad moonlights from his job as chief operating officer and general manager at the prestigious East Lake Club in Atlanta, and helps his dad Carl make dill pickles. And a jar of Parker's Pickles, with their never-to-be-revealed secret ingredient, is usually considered payment enough to get some of the game's elite down to Florence. "When Zach Johnson came down in 2007, just two months after winning the Masters, he thought he was entitled to a second jar," recalls Chad, a twenty-plus year veteran of East Lake, smiling at the memory. "We told him, sorry—one to a customer. But he took it well!"

Despite the pickle paucity, Zach keeps coming back. He knows, as do all his fellow professionals, that marinated cucumbers are nice, but supporting the Healing Place is really the key ingredient.

For more information visit: www.thehealingplaceinfo.org

The Hundred Hole Hike

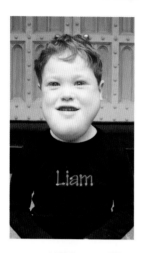

There is tremendous variety in the events found within these pages. There is a diversity of causes, geographies, histories, sizes, formats and revenue streams, to name but a few differing aspects of charity golf. But there is nothing remotely like the Hundred Hole Hike, the brainchild of a Chicago banking executive named Jim Colton.

Colton's initial impetus was to walk, play and finish as many holes as possible in a single day to raise funds for a caddy who had become paralyzed from the chest down in a skiing accident. The venue was Ballyneal, a national destination golf club in remote Holyoke, Colorado, about three hours northeast of Denver. Though Colton was a member of the club, he wasn't acquainted with the injured caddy, Ben Cox. "Though I didn't know him I still wanted to help," explains Colton. "I figured if I sent an email to forty of my golf friends, people would pitch in a dollar or two a hole. For whatever reason, the event just really struck a chord with the golf community. I walked 155 holes that day and we wound up raising more than $110,000."

From that seemingly one-off act of altruism in 2011, the Hundred Hole Hike was born. The goal of the organization is to take the same passion and energy that fueled what became known as the Ben Cox 155 to a grander scale. Instead of one golfer at one club for one cause, the event has grown to include numerous golfers at various clubs around the world, all walking and finishing at least one hundred holes to raise money for a variety of worthwhile causes as chosen by the individual hiker. It takes a special breed of passionate golfer to raise funds by committing to walk and play all day long. I know from personal experience; I took on the challenge and participated in a Hundred Hole Hike in 2012.

I was one of more than sixty golfers who collectively raised over a quarter of a million dollars for various causes that year. More than eighty trudged the dawn-to-dusk miles the year after that, more than ninety the year after that, with the fundraising rising commensurately. Total dollars collected are now into the seven figures.

The money raised by all of these intrepid walkers goes

to worthy causes as varied as the colors of the rainbow. There are the customary medical research organizations looking to fight diseases like Alzheimer's, cancer, diabetes, multiple sclerosis, muscular dystrophy, Parkinson's, leukemia and lymphoma. There are "brand name" causes represented, like Wounded Warriors, Habitat for Humanity, the Smile Train, Big Brothers and Big Sisters, St. Jude Children's Research, Ronald McDonald House, Special Olympics, and Susan G. Komen. And as might be expected from the crème de la crème of golf fanatics that are drawn to an exploit like this, golf-specific charities are championed; organizations like The First Tee, Evans Scholars and various other scholarship programs also garner support.

The cause I chose to hike for was more esoteric. Liam's Land is a non-profit that seeks to find a cure for a little-known but insidious disease called lymphatic malformation, or LM. Usually striking children, these lymphatic malformations are abnormal channels and cysts filled with clear lymphatic fluid, usually in the neck area or near the armpit. The disease can cause swelling of the tongue, leading to difficulty breathing, speaking and eating. It often causes facial deformity, and sometimes necessitates the insertion of a tracheotomy tube. I hiked for the Steffen family of Savannah, Georgia, whose five-year-old son

Liam has undergone nearly a dozen surgical procedures for this affliction. His parents, Joe and Janet, started the non-profit hoping to raise research funds.

Because little Liam has had to endure a tough road from day one, I was prepared to take a tough road myself for at least one day. On the morning of my Hundred Hole Hike, at an hour when most men are lathering on shaving cream, I was turning the same trick, head-to-toe, with an industrial-size bottle of sunscreen. These hikes generally occur around the summer solstice, when daylight is most abundant. The problem is that in the South Carolina lowcountry, late June can mean triple digit heat indices. I poked my head outdoors just after dawn broke, and was first hit with the stultifying warmth and heavy air that felt like a cross between cobwebs and cotton candy. Despite the inherent lack of elevation of the topography, I knew the day ahead was going to be an uphill battle.

People ask what it's like to walk and golf your ball for over twelve hours in hundred-degree heat. It's not for the faint of heart, and on the same topic, fainting is always a possibility. I had some advantages and disadvantages in comparison to my hiking brethren.

- Advantage: the course was walker-friendly, an old-school layout, very flat, with short distances between greens and tees.
- Disadvantage: at age 51, I was probably fifteen years older than the average hiker, and twenty-plus years older than many.
- Advantage: other than playing through one foursome one time, I literally had the course to myself the entire day.
- Disadvantage: nobody else was playing because it was like an infrared sauna out there.
- Advantage: while many hikers carried their own bags, at least part of the time, I had a rotating series of caddies. I may be crazy, but I'm not insane. I went through those bag-toters like Liz Taylor went through husbands- quickly, casually, and with little emotional attachment.

During thirteen on-course hours, I made enough costume changes to rival Bette Midler on Broadway, going through three shirts, several pairs of shorts, five pairs of socks, and changing golf shoes three or four times. As for sustenance, it was mostly water, a little coconut water, a few bananas, a handful of cookies, a small bag of almonds, a couple of energy-gel packets, and eventually some fruit. During a lunch break I took time for a sandwich and a shower. Both were needed in equal measure.

Trudging up the clubhouse stairs at day's end, it was gratifying to receive a lovely and enthusiastic ovation by a twelve-person dinner party, still enjoying cocktail hour, who came out to greet me on the porch. Far better than the warm applause and photo barrage was the fact that all of these folks met little Liam Steffen and his parents, who were there to support my effort along with his Pippie Longstocking look-alike sister Amalie.

The difference between the Hundred Hole Hike and almost any other golf charity event one can name is that instead of supporting a predetermined cause, the player chooses something they care deeply about. Then after a series of solicitation emails, phone calls and face-to-face encounters, the fundraising begins in earnest. One step, one hole, one mile, one round at a time. Hundreds of swings beget thousands of dollars. At day's end, the feeling of accomplishment, both for dollars raised and energy expended, leaves the hiker lightheaded. Janet Steffen put it best. The founder of Liam's Land wisely remarked at day's end, "pain is temporary, satisfaction lasts forever!"

**For more information visit: www.hundredholehike.com
or: liamsland.org**

The National Kidney Foundation of Louisiana

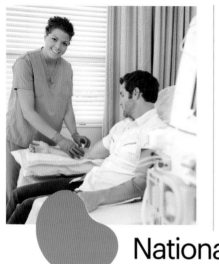

One needn't be as logical as Star Trek's Mr. Spock or have the deductive reasoning of Sherlock Holmes to understand why Louisiana has the highest rate of kidney disease in the nation.

This so-called "silent killer" is a direct result of high blood pressure and diabetes. These all-too-common health concerns are themselves a direct result of poor eating, smoking, excessive partying, and other problematic habits. So ipso facto, the "laissez les bon temps roulez" (let the good times roll) lifestyle that is one of

National Kidney Foundation™

the hallmarks of Louisiana life have, over the long term, resulted in some serious health consequences for far too many of the state's citizenry.

"It often comes down to family history, poor choices and what might be described as an indulgent lifestyle," begins Torie Kranze, the longtime CEO of the National Kidney Foundation of Louisiana.

It's not just a Louisiana problem. One of three individuals nationwide are at risk for kidney disease, but might not know it. However the problem is exacerbated on a per-capita basis throughout the state known as Sportsman's Paradise. There are nearly half a million Louisianans with kidney disease, more than nine thousand residents on dialysis, and some eighteen hundred awaiting a kidney transplant. (There are in excess of 100,000 awaiting transplants nationwide.) "Kidney disease kills more people in our state than either breast cancer or prostate cancer," continues Kranze, who has two decades of tenure with the foundation.

Kidneys filter the blood, keep blood pressure stable, keep the right amount of fluids in the body, and help produce red blood cells. Blood and urine tests are the way to monitor kidney function. Too much protein in the urine is an ominous sign, and a blood test estimates the filtration rate of the kidneys. "Early stage sufferers don't have conspicuous symptoms," states Kranze. "It's only later on when the urine is too dark, swelling commences in the hands and feet, or lower back pain manifests that it gets discovered. Those past the age of sixty, Native Americans and African Americans are particularly susceptible to kidney disease."

The National Kidney Foundation of Louisiana has modified its approach in recent years. They were originally focused almost exclusively on the three types of patient on dialysis, which is the protocol when kidney function ceases and the blood must be cleaned and purified via machine. Full dialysis requires up to six hours a day, three times a week at a medical facility. Home dialysis is done with a bag of fluid at home, just a few hours every day, eliminating the need for transportation to and from the kidney center. The third option is an in-home dialysis machine, which requires the help of a caregiver to help operate the medical equipment and supervise the patient.

With the recent epidemic of kidney disease, the National Kidney Foundation of Louisiana has refocused on education and prevention, as opposed to the last resort of dialysis. "We do early testing, early education and take pre-emptive action to stem the tide in advance of the full onset of the disease," states Kranze, who has lived in New Orleans for more than twenty-five years.

With advances in laparoscopic surgery and more effective anti-rejection drugs, more doctors are opting for the preemptive transplantation of kidneys, avoiding dialysis completely. "While once the protocol was to go on dialysis and do a transplant as a last resort, nowadays more doctors feel the transplant offers both a better long term solution, and a better quality of life for patients, who don't have to remain tethered to a dialysis machine. The bigger problem remains finding donors."

Increasing the donor list is the most pressing problem facing Kranze and her staff of five. They deal with persistent myths that suppress the motivation to donate kidneys or other vital organs among the populace at large. These include thinking that one must pay to donate organs, that doctors won't expend their full energies to resuscitate an organ donor, that wealth or celebrity allows the privileged few to cut the line to receive organs, or that religious reasons preclude them from doing so. According to the CEO, all these reasons are fallacious, with no basis in truth.

The National Kidney Foundation of Louisiana is particularly proud of their summer camp, which brings together young people from Louisiana and Texas. "Often these kids feel isolated," states Kranze. "They might not know other kids on dialysis, or who've had or are awaiting transplants. This is an incredible bonding experience, with deep friendships formed among those who might otherwise never have the chance to meet."

Kidneys in the Classroom is another prevention-based program, geared towards grade school kids, but with the added bonus of reaching the adults in their lives. They teach basic science to the children in school and attempt to imprint healthy lifestyle choices, with the underlying hope that the kids will discuss what they've learned at home. "This is an innovative way for us to get the message out about healthy lifestyle choices from the kids to the adults, as opposed to the other way around," explains Kranze.

It is for all these reasons that the National Kidney Foundation of Louisiana relies on not just one or two, but five different golf fundraisers statewide, from April through November every year. New Orleans, Baton Rouge, Squire Creek,

Lafayette and Alexandria are the locales, and most every event has been raising funds and awareness concurrently for at least two decade's duration.

The first event was initiated in Alexandria by a non-playing nephrologist. He thought a golf event would get more people paying attention to their kidney health. The Baton Rouge event was also initiated by a non-golfer, the wife of an avid player who had a family history of kidney disease. "That event has provided publicity, awareness and year-round community support that wouldn't have developed without the golf tournament," states Kranze, who, because of the ubiquity of these fundraising events has become a golfer herself.

Squire Creek is a highly acclaimed destination golf club midway between Shreveport and Monroe. Their event honors the memory of Clarke M. Williams, founder of the telecommunications giant CenturyTel, who died while on dialysis back in 2002. Lafayette's event is the brainchild of another non-playing nephrologist, and the biggest of the bunch is of course in New Orleans. Their gala dinner attracts eight hundred altruistic yet fun-loving souls, dwarfing the full-field golf tournament the following day.

"Back in 2005, the weather was looking dicey, so we had to cancel and reschedule our New Orleans tournament," concludes Kranze, shaking her head at the irony. "Wouldn't you know, we were slated to have our fundraiser on the day that Hurricane Katrina hit."

Needless to say there was no iteration in 2005, but they came back stronger than ever in 2006. Just like the good times, ubiquitous in New Orleans and throughout the state, the National Kidney Foundation of Louisiana rolls on.

Mercedes-Benz Superdome

For more information visit: www.kidneyla.org

Lisa Beth Gerstman Foundation

LISA BETH GERSTMAN FOUNDATION

Eleven-year-old Lisa Beth Gerstman, a joyful child, energetic, 'good as gold,' according to her parents Harvey and Carol, would soon be entering her middle school years. But first, summertime meant summer camp near her Long Island home. In July, when her Hillel day camp announced an overnight trip to Pennsylvania's Hershey Park she was ecstatic, although her enthusiasm was tempered because her nine-year-old brother Dan wasn't old enough to enjoy the exotic field trip in that summer of 1970.

"The camp bus was outside Allentown, slid on a patch of wet road and tumbled end over end, fifty feet down an embankment," recalls Dan, his tone morose some forty-five years later. "Seven kids were killed, including our Lisa. Not a day goes by that I don't think of her, and mourn our family's heartache."

The Gerstman family, shattered by the loss, soldiered on as best they could. Linda, a true blessing, completed the family, joining Dan and his little brother Brad as the baby sister.

Harvey, a lifelong athlete turned salesman, threw himself into his work, and began his own Manufacturers Representative sales agency in 1978. As his three children grew to adulthood, eventually joining the firm, they followed the example of the dawn-to-dusk work ethic of their dad and founder, and over time the business became a notable success. The Gerstman Group and its sister retail services company Quest Service Group, represent manufacturers in the home channel industry and provide vital retail services in all fifty states for major players like Home

Depot and Ace Hardware.

The Lisa Beth Gerstman Foundation was initiated in 2002, more than thirty years after its namesake's passing, when Dan, now in his 40s, felt compelled to make a donation to the Cross Island YMCA in the borough of Queens, NYC. He wanted to help kids attend summer camp. "It was something I felt strongly about, could afford to do, and wanted to do in Lisa's name," recounts the father of four.

Asked to join the YMCA's Board, he met a silver-haired aquatics coach named Jean Dattner, who both enlightened him and sharpened his philanthropic focus. "Talking about some of the physically challenged kids she taught swimming, Jean matter-of-factly told me these kids had nothing to do all summer but sit at home, waiting for school to begin. I realized that raising funds so these special needs kids could attend summer camp; paying for additional staff, equipment and transportation, was the perfect vehicle to focus the Foundation's efforts. And since we met, Jean has been with us every step of the way."

As Brad Gerstman eloquently points out, "Kids that have learning or physical disabilities or other special needs can get the care and special attention they need during the school year, but we came to learn they were virtually shut out come summer. We realized the perfect way to honor Lisa's memory was to begin this program as a family."

From a single YMCA in Queens, the Lisa Beth Gerstman Foundation has expanded to include more than fifteen camps around metropolitan New York, including all five boroughs. Before the golf outing debuted in 2007, virtually all the Foundation's funding came from the Gerstman family and a few select friends. But thanks to the unbridled success of the golf event, held at Long Island's Glen Head Country Club, the overall monies raised now dwarf the continued steady contributions of Lisa's immediate family. As Brad Gerstman proudly states, "The foundation has doubled, even tripled in size due in large part to the golf outing." The Gerstman family, including cousin Gregg, loyal company employees Matilde and Roberta, and event planner Cindy Mardenfeld from Infinity Relations make up the brain trust of the golf committee.

A significant factor in the golf event's continued success is the support of Home Depot. "On the one hand it's amazing that Home Depot supports the foundation to the significant degree they do, because we sell to them, not vice-versa, which means we have zero leverage," states Linda Gerstman. "On the other hand, because Home Depot makes a point of hiring workers that might be physically or mentally disadvantaged, they completely understand our mission." Joe McFarland, a top-level Home Depot executive, has been particularly supportive, and was one of the tournament's inaugural honorees.

Explaining the outing's success, Linda Gerstman continues, "We just don't skimp. It's not an inexpensive day by any means, but all first-class, from the pre-tournament brunch to the top-notch golf venue, then the cocktail hour, the dinner, the raffle with amazing and valuable prizes, people are always astounded by the level of hospitality we provide."

The attendees are also touched by the fact that some of the YMCA campers are present to give out gift bags in the morning, while other campers circulate with their families during dinner, letting the donors see for themselves the types of well-deserving children their hard-earned dollars support.

In short, the Lisa Beth Gerstman Foundation provides grants to existing summer camps so they are better able to serve the needs of a physically and intellectually challenged population. Kids confined to wheelchairs, those that might be hearing or sight impaired, or somewhere on the autism spectrum, can now enjoy the sports, games, activities, events, and enduring friendships that made Lisa Beth herself such an enthusiastic and fun-loving camper before the tragic bus accident cut her young life short all those many years ago.

For more information visit: www.lisabethgerstman.org

The 'Life Event' LPGA Pros in the Fight to Eradicate Breast Cancer

Heather Farr was just a whisker over five feet tall, practically as light as her given name. Despite her slight stature, she amazed and impressed her collegiate golf peers and eventually her colleagues on the LPGA Tour with how much she squeezed out of her golf game.

By the same token, though she was just twenty-eight when breast cancer cheated her from her just due, Farr squeezed a tremendous amount out of life in the short time she had. Hers was a life full of friendship, laughter, charity, romance, family, golf excellence, and an unwavering commitment to her craft. It's a testament to the buoyancy of her spirit and the profound impact she had on those who knew her and loved her that her memory lives to this day, more than twenty years after her passing.

Multiple millions have been raised in her honor to not only combat the scourge of breast cancer, but to imprint on young women everywhere to be cognizant of any changes to their own bodies, and to become the best advocate possible for their own health. Despite the vast potential she had to become a successful professional golfer, this is Farr's most enduring legacy.

"I first met Heather when she was an undergrad at Arizona State, and she would come watch our LPGA event in Phoenix," reminisces Val Skinner, a twenty-year veteran of the Tour. Skinner couldn't have predicted that these casual encounters would lead to an enduring friendship, and in time, lead the six-time LPGA tournament winner to become a tireless advocate and fundraising whirlwind for women's health issues.

"She was tiny, but mighty," recalls Skinner, who became something of a mentor to Farr. "I

was always long off the tee and occasionally wild. Heather wanted to add length, but was proud of her accuracy. We each wanted what the other had! But beyond golf she was fun to be with, was such a positive person, exuded confidence in an appealing way, had a great sense of humor, very likable. She was a special young woman."

Skinner began to invite Farr to participate in some grassroots charity events to better women's lives, and Heather began to develop a passion and connection of her own for the cause. The sad irony is that it wasn't too long thereafter that Skinner, Beth Daniel, Nancy Lopez, Meg Mallon, Karrie Webb and many other LPGA luminaries were helping raise funds for Farr's medical treatments.

"When Heather first went back to visit her doctor in Phoenix in 1989 after she felt an abnormality, I was as casual as most of our peers," recalls Skinner, who spent a dozen years as a Golf Channel commentator after her regular tour career wound down and still plays the Legends Tour. "I remember telling her not to worry, at her age it was probably a calcification or some other minor matter, and I'd see her at the next Tour stop. The possibility of breast cancer didn't seem reasonable."

As her health worsened, Farr developed a unique ability to comfort others, who felt so badly about her dire straits. "We had an event in Nashville to raise money for her treatments. It's not easy to describe, but when she spoke that evening she was so present, so grateful, so composed in the face of her mortality." Skinner equates Farr's personal resolve to the qualities that made her such a formidable golfer. "It was inner strength, self-belief, confidence and hopefulness. She talked candidly about her circumstances not for pity, but to potentially help others. Those of us who were lucky enough to hear her speak that evening will never forget it."

Heather married a PING representative

named Goran Lingmerth during her illness. Though she might have wished for more privacy as she struggled, she engaged the media regularly. She was intent on hammering home the point that young women need to be proactive in their self-screenings, and not assume that their youth and apparent health will somehow protect them from the ubiquity of the disease.

Val Skinner visited her in the Arizona hospital to offer a prayer just prior to Thanksgiving in 1993. By now Farr wasn't able to communicate; she was sedated, receiving palliative care. Skinner flew across the continent to her New Jersey home, and was told her friend, a few months away from her twenty-ninth birthday, had passed during the night.

"One can't overstate the impact Heather had on all of us on the LPGA Tour, which is really a family," continues Skinner. "She found love, kept working on her game, would participate in golf outings where she could, lived in the moment. She caused an epic wave of change across the Tour in how we thought about our own health. At its heart it was due to our admiration and respect for her, and how she conducted herself, and educated all of us by her example."

In memory of her friend, Skinner soon got involved raising money for breast cancer at various events around New Jersey. Her ardent fundraising, half a million dollars in total, led to her receiving an award from the Susan G. Komen Foundation at the LPGA's fiftieth anniversary gala in 1999. And that was really just the beginning.

In what Skinner still considers a moment of divine intervention, she was seated at the gala next to a young woman named Diane Balma. An attorney by profession, she was twice misdiagnosed with what was actually breast cancer. This profound life event led her to change direction and come to work for the Komen Foundation as their director of public policy. "Within moments of meeting we agreed that she would help me with a young women's initiative, and I would somehow find the money to fund it."

Thanks in large part to Skinner's founding of perhaps the most prestigious LPGA-centric charity golf event in the nation, filled with luminaries past and present, more than ten million dollars has been raised for breast cancer research, treatment, and education through the Val Skinner Foundation.

Since the inaugural LIFE event in 2000, there's been great progress made on a variety of fronts. A few highlights include the opening of the LIFE Center at The Cancer Institute of New Jersey on the campus of Rutgers University in 2002. It serves as the laboratory for the development and evaluation of novel educational tools and strategies for community education of young women. LIFE has also made generous grants to the Precision Medicine Initiative at the same institute, which helps identify specific mutations in the body.

Komen on the Go, a national education campaign that featured two large pink tour buses, traveled nationwide to college campuses and community events during its eight-year run, educating young women regarding self-screening, healthy lifestyle choices. Over the years this program reached millions of individuals, encouraging them to be proactive.

Young Women Walking was launched with LIFE funds. The program works in concert with the popular Komen three-day, sixty-mile fundraising walks. As exciting as anything else is their BIOCONECT interactive platform, a supplementary curriculum for biology and science classes that is going nationwide. This is a learning module on cancer genetics available to millions of educators and thirty-five million students.

Struck down in her prime, Heather's early demise was a crushing blow to her husband, family, friends and the entire golf world. But thanks to the subsequent dedication and tenacity by Val Skinner and numerous others colleagues and friends, now millions of young women and teens have the tools and information to stay self-aware. Heather died young, but many thousands will live rich, full lives. There is some comfort in that.

For more information
visit: www.valskinnerfoundation.org

Lurie Children's Pro Amateur Golf Championship

LURIE CHILDREN'S PRO AMATEUR GOLF CHAMPIONSHIP

In Pasadena, California, there's long been a college football tilt contested on New Year's Day. The Rose Bowl is located just a smidge over two thousand miles from the Lurie Children's Pro Amateur Golf Championship in Chicago. The former is a world famous bowl game. The latter is an astonishingly successful fundraiser. And it's no stretch to refer to both of these iconic events by the same moniker: "The Granddaddy of Them All."

When the Pro Amateur Golf Championship began in 1961, gas was a quarter a gallon, the average new house cost little more than twelve grand, and soon-to-be golf icon Jack Nicklaus had no children in the house and no majors on the mantle. Over time, Nicklaus collected eighteen majors, five kids and nearly two-dozen grandchildren. The Pro Am has flourished commensurately.

David Gorter, former chairman of the event's men's golf committee and a Pro Am participant for more than twenty-five years, shares some history: "Back in the old days, when the nearby Western Open was part of the PGA Tour schedule, we could attract the likes of Jack Nicklaus, Arnold Palmer and Lee Trevino to play in our event." The Pro Am switched the "pro" focus of their event to top-notch club professionals as tour stars became more costly to woo. A prescient move, as the Western

Open disappeared completely after 2006. This is just one example of the flexibility and forward thinking that has allowed the Lurie Children's Pro Amateur Golf Championship to continuously prosper for more than fifty-five years.

The tournament's antiquity is a relative matter, as the hospital itself has been in operation since the 1880s. Its current iteration dates from 2012, having moved from the Lincoln Park neighborhood to the Streeterville section of downtown Chicago, in a gleaming, twenty-three-story building, likely the tallest children's hospital in the world, not to mention one of the best.

More than 174,000 children are treated annually, from newborns to collegiate undergrads, at what was for many years known as Children's Memorial Hospital, and is now officially known as Ann & Robert H. Lurie Children's Hospital of Chicago. The facility has nearly three hundred beds, with more than 1,300 pediatric doctors providing care and research in seventy subspecialties. Among other areas of expertise, Lurie Children's reputation with gastroenterology, neurology, urology, cancer, blood disorders and kidney ailments is second to none. Lauren Gorter has served on the hospital's Founders' Board for two decades, including a recent stint as president. "By almost any measure: size, patient visits, quality of care, reputation, we are one of the finest children's hospitals in the nation. We pride ourselves on treating all children in need, despite the fact that more than fifty percent of our patients are on Medicaid, or have no means to pay. That's why consistent fundraising is vital to our mission-so we can continue to provide excellent medical care to all."

"All told we receive donations in excess of fifty million dollars annually," adds Katie Spieth, who has a decade of tenure at Lurie Children's Foundation, the hospital's charitable arm. "In addition to our generous individual, corporate and planned gifts, we have nearly 250 fundraisers annually, of all sizes and scopes. Many of these are smaller, casual events, perhaps something initiated by a local Girl Scouts troop. However we have nearly a dozen marquee events on the fundraising calendar, and the Pro Amateur Golf Championship is certainly in that category. It is a critical element in terms of generating funds, goodwill and awareness of our hospital, and the great work that's done there."

"It's really amazing the way our tournament brings people together every year," continues Lauren Gorter." It's a great connector, both for first-timers, and those who've played for decades. The city's business leaders, philanthropists, doctors, parents of patients, former patients, golf-lovers, our professionals, a wonderfully diverse group of individuals coming together every year for this extremely worthy cause. The atmosphere is very convivial, spirits are high, and we have such a rich tradition to celebrate."

" It's an action-packed day, from 7 AM until 7 PM," offers David Gorter. "We pair a professional with four amateurs during both a morning and afternoon wave of tee times. The fact that the prestigious Onwentsia Club has been our host practically every year since the beginning is a tremendous plus. It's one of Chicago's finest clubs, and people love the opportunity to play there."

When a tournament spans the length of ten presidential administrations, it spawns weighty family legacies. There are a number of Chicago-area families that have played for decades with at least three, if not four, generations having participated. "My family is a classic example," continues David Gorter, "My grandfather played, my father plays, I play and one of my sons now plays. This kind of support is very unique and is not something you see at most charity golf events; it speaks to the deep ties many have with the Hospital and its mission."

In lieu of tour pros, the Pro Am invites some of the finest club and teaching professionals from around the nation. They play for a cash prize among themselves on the Sunday preceding the event. The tournament festivities tee off at a much-anticipated dinner where hundreds of players, benefactors and patrons gather for an evening's worth of festivities prior to the Pro Am on Monday. "The original event in 1961 raised about $65,000 for the hospital," concludes Katie Spieth. "Nowadays we raise in excess of one and a half million dollars annually, so it's easy to see how the golf tournament has added tens of millions of dollars to our bottom line over the decades."

There's no precise way of gauging what might be the oldest, continuously running charity golf tournament. There's no reliable census data, nor historical record. Suffice it to say that the Lurie Children's Pro Amateur Golf Championship is among the truly venerable. To sum it up, one can repurpose a famous riposte from a seen-it-all football coach of yesteryear. "I'm not going to say he's in a class by himself," offered the coach, when asked about his superstar running back. "But whatever class he's in, it doesn't take long to call the roll."

Same story with the Lurie Children's Pro Amateur Golf Championship, an event that imbues class, and well over a half-century later, continues to roll.

For more information visit: www.luriechildrens.org

The LWGA's Golfing for a Cure

People who know the game well can deduce pretty quickly that the biggest women's golf association in the United States is the LPGA—Ladies Professional Golf Association. But not one in a hundred could fathom a guess as to the second largest. That would be the LWGA—the Landings Women's Golf Association, found at the Landings Club on bucolic Skidaway Island, Georgia, just outside Savannah, with a membership of about five hundred.

It's not surprising the LWGA is so formidable, because the Landings Club is as well. Four thousand acres, six championship golf courses, four clubhouses, over thirty tennis courts and two marinas are just the tip of the iceberg at this Disneyland for adults. And when the women of the LWGA set their mind to raise funds for cancer, their results are just as impressive as the island paradise they call home.

"The LWGA is a special group of dedicated women," offers Landings Club Executive Director Steven Freund. "It's not surprising they put forth the type of effort they do for cancer research. This entire island is populated with committed, generous and civic-minded individuals. I suppose part of it is that they feel extremely fortunate to have found themselves ensconced on this wonderfully tranquil island, with the salt marshes, long-range water views, shadowed biking and walking paths shaded by centuries-old live oaks, and literally dozens of first-class amenities at their disposal. They are lucky to call a community of this caliber home, and feel as though they are obligated to give back to those who are in need."

Marianne Kosiewicz offers a perfect example. She is a recent chairman of the LWGA's Golfing for a Cure fundraiser, and was a high-level committee member for several years prior.

"It's the most fantastic place I've ever had the chance to live in the United States," offer Kosiewicz emphatically. "All the amazing amenities aside, the natural beauty of the island is overwhelming, but it's not manicured or artificial. The city of Savannah is so close by, with its inherent charm, quirkiness, history and art scene. Considered separately, perhaps neither the island nor the city would have prompted us to move here. But in tandem it is a remarkable place to live. I had a fulfilling career in academia," recalls the former Associate Dean of Admissions at the prestigious University of Virginia, "and my husband John had a leadership role in military intelligence. There are hundreds of people and couples we've met here from all walks of life who are incredibly accomplished, whose career stories are so interesting. Despite the tranquility and beauty, the residents of Skidaway Island and the Landings make this an energizing place to be."

There's energy to burn when more than two-thirds of the LWGA come out to support Golfing for a Cure every April. "We have dozens of social and competitive events on our annual calendar," relates Kosiewicz. "But many members only come out for this one thing. Obviously they feel very strongly about raising funds for cancer research, so they pay their annual dues, the one hundred dollar entry fee for the tournament, and the cost of the lunch just to have access to this one outing."

Once again, the power of numbers helps make the Landings Club tick. Modest though the entry fee may be (other events in this book cost ten, twenty, even fifty times as much) the LWGA still nets well in excess of fifty thousand dollars annually for Savannah's Anderson Cancer Institute, and has donated more than a half-million dollars over time. They do it with hole sponsors, traditional games of chance, and even a unique art raffle. "We have a vibrant artistic community on Skidaway Island," offers Linda Rich, the 2016 event chairman. "Our art raffle is unusual because players buy chances only on the piece or pieces they are interested in, which prevents someone from winning a painting or sculpture that they aren't enamored with, or might not fit their home decor."

Rich has long been enamored with the island she calls home and the women she interacts with, both on and off the golf course. "I got involved in a leadership capacity at the LWGA because they're an impressive group. Not only who they are and what they've accomplished, but their passion to fight cancer."

"Like many people, when I first came over the bridge spanning the Intracoastal Waterway to Skidaway Island, I could feel this place was special. It's beyond the beauty out your front door. It's also the fact that whatever you want to do, whether it's art, or gardening, or tennis, golf or bocce, there are dozens if not

hundreds of people who enjoy doing the same thing. It's an instant network if you choose to take advantage of it."

The LWGA has certainly taken advantage of its proximity to Savannah's renowned Anderson Cancer Institute. When Golfing for a Cure debuted around the turn of the century it was originally affiliated with the American Cancer Society. But in 2004 they localized their efforts to the Anderson Cancer Institute, one of the finest research and treatment centers in the Southeast. "The cause resonates so deeply with our membership that we get this remarkably high turnout every year," continues Kosiewicz. "We fill three of our courses to capacity, and the only reason the event isn't larger is because our ballroom cannot hold more players and guests. As it is, we have close to three hundred players taking part."

Although monies raised help fund research into a wide spectrum of cancers, a certain sum is directed towards the breast-specific intraoperative radiation therapy. This technique radiates a tumor just one time during surgery, and spares the patient from returning to the doctor's office daily for weeks at a time, which for many years has been the standard protocol in treating this ubiquitous disease.

Both Rich and Kosiewicz are quick to state that while chairman is the most integral position at the annual fundraiser, there are more than a dozen different committee members filling a variety of essential roles to make this one-day extravaganza click. Be it advertising, registration, table decor, raffle tickets, accounting, or numerous other vital tasks, these women know from long experience it takes a village. And there are very few "villages" with the charm, beauty, and astonishing number of highly motivated and accomplished residents as those living, working, volunteering and playing at the one-of-a-kind Landings Club on Skidaway Island, Georgia.

For more information visit: www.lwga.net

The Annual Martin Klaiber Memorial Golf Tournament

ANNUAL
MARTIN
KLAIBER
MEMORIAL GOLF TOURNAMENT

It's long been said that life begins at forty. This well-known phrase is actually the title of, among other things, a John Lennon song, a Will Rogers movie, a self-help book from the 30s, and a Chinese television series.

Sadly, life ended at forty for Martin Klaiber. In autumn of 2013 he was the sole fatality in a multi-car collision on a dusky byway in the D.C. suburb of Leesburg, Virginia. But thanks to the ongoing love and dedication of his wife, Stephanie, and their respective families, Martin's memory and his zest for life live on.

It was an excruciating decision to take him off life support a week after he was airlifted from the scene of the accident. Ultimately, the choice to do so was based on two factors. The first was that the numerous medical opinions rendered were bleak. Martin was unlikely to emerge from his coma, or ever be able to breathe, speak or eat again. The other was the fact that he was a committed organ and tissue donor. His organs were weakening, and for others to benefit a judgment needed to be made posthaste.

"On a ventilator, or with a tracheotomy tube, the body's organs don't function as naturally or normally as when a person is truly living," explains Stephanie. "It was ultimately my decision to take him off of life support. However, it was only after consulting with both of our families. It was the hardest thing I've ever done, but the blessing was that Martin saved three other lives that very night. Both of his kidneys and his liver went to critical care patients in the D.C. area."

Within a year, he had helped save three additional lives, including two newborn baby girls, born with heart defects, who survived thanks to heart tissue harvested from his body. The irony was not lost on those who knew him well. Martin Klaiber

was all heart.

"What can I say? He was the love of my life, my partner, my best friend, my soul mate," sighs Stephanie. "Nobody's perfect, but he was perfect for me. Part of me died with him when we let him go." Martin was an entrepreneur, in business development and sales, with a multi-faceted career track that allowed him to showcase his best attribute: people skills. "He lit up a room when he walked in, his smile was contagious," recalls Stephanie, smiling herself at the thought. "He wanted to know everyone's name, where they were from. He marched to his own beat, didn't really care what others thought, which was the main reason he had countless friends, colleagues, golf buddies. He had more networks than you could imagine. I still hear from people whose names I don't recognize more than a year after his passing."

After the auto accident and its heartbreaking aftermath, Stephanie took a long hiatus from her marketing career. When she returned to work months later, she quickly realized she had lost her drive. "We were both career-oriented, hoping to retire early and travel the world. When I went back to work it was uncomfortable. People didn't know what to say, how to act. The truth is there's nothing they can say or do to ease the pain and loss. It was as if I was wearing a scarlet letter, and it was just a few months later I left my job, and began to concentrate on building a non-profit foundation to honor my husband's memory and legacy."

Golf tournaments are a tried and true method to raise funds, and for Stephanie it was a natural fit. Martin was a certifiable golf nut. He adored the game, played and practiced as much as possible, and was always tinkering with both his equipment and his swing, searching for the game's ineffable "secret".

The first charity tournament, contested in 2014, raised $21,000. The seven thousand allocated to each of the three beneficiaries continued the eerie theme of the number seven throughout the nightmarish ordeal of the accident and the consequences. "We celebrated our seventh anniversary in the hospital," recounts Stephanie, thinking back to that surreal week while he hovered between life and death. "We had lived in our home for seven years. We had our rescue dog, Chelsea, for seven years. Martin's favorite club was his seven-iron. My stepdad opened one of Martin's favorite books at home while he was in the hospital on life support. Seven of his business cards fell out. The priest who read his last rites told me he had been ordained for seven years. When the final fundraising numbers came in, I felt that it was practically predetermined. I'm so glad we could give each of these three wonderful organizations a substantial check, and look forward to giving them larger donations in the future."

The three organizations supported by the tournament's proceeds are the Loudon First Responders Foundation, the Washington Regional Transplant

Community, and Tails of Hope.

"The first responders at least gave us a sense of hope. They gave me a warm body for that final week, instead of a cold one," relates Stephanie. "They do wonderful work, they are the first on the scene and the first to leave the scene, and consequently get little recognition. The foundation raises scholarship funds for the kids of first responders as well as helps the first responders and their families when they are injured in the line of duty."

The second beneficiary is the Washington Regional Transplant Community, the local arm of the national organization Donate Life America. "It's a wonderful organization above and beyond the fact they help facilitate the harvesting and transportation of vital organs. They also offer counseling and empathy. I am still in contact with the staff, and they continue to help me process my grief long after Martin's passing."

Lastly, Tails of Hope rescues dogs that are stranded, abandoned or facing euthanasia, and finds them permanent homes. It differs from the ASPCA in that there are no kennels involved. Dogs are placed with foster families until permanent homes can be found. "We have a rescue dog ourselves. Chelsea was Martin's Christmas present to me when we were first married," concludes Stephanie. "Although we have ten nieces and nephews, we don't have children of our own. Chelsea is part of the family, and I understand how vital the work that Tails of Hope does in helping dogs find their families and vice-versa. It's an organization that understands that owning a dog can really enhance your life. "

Any way you describe him, the word "life" would likely be part of the script. Life of the party, full of life, a strong life force, lifelong friend, larger than life, etc. So it's only appropriate that Martin Klaiber, in the prime of life when he passed, was able to prolong and enhance the lives of a half-dozen other fortunate souls after his own ended far too soon.

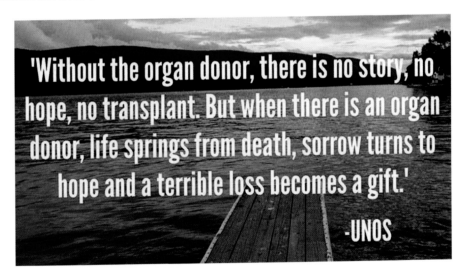

'Without the organ donor, there is no story, no hope, no transplant. But when there is an organ donor, life springs from death, sorrow turns to hope and a terrible loss becomes a gift.'

-UNOS

For more information visit: www.givingandsavinglives.com

The Matthew Renk Foundation

Think Grey. It's not as catchy a phrase, nor nearly as ubiquitous, as 'Think Pink,' the rallying cry for breast cancer. However Jackie and Dave Renk, of Bucks County, Pennsylvania, went to great lengths to trademark the expression, which reminds us to be aware of brain cancer, the most lethal cancer scourge for young people twenty and under. They hope the catchphrase leads to greater awareness over time. But their deepest wish is that they never had to trademark it at all.

In 2008, when their thirteen-year-old son Matthew complained of a headache, his mom wasn't alarmed. She just got him some aspirin. But the headache persisted, and several days later on the school bus the nascent eighth-grader became violently ill. The emergency room cat scan that followed was swift, decisive and cruel: medulla blastoma—a brain tumor.

"Matthew was just a toddler when I got the job at Lookaway," begins his father Dave, who still serves as the only superintendant this prestigious golf club in pastoral Buckingham, Pennsylvania has ever known. "He literally grew up on the course, and loved to help me however and whenever he could: cutting, watering, weeding, upholding the very high maintenance standards we have. Everyone associated with the club—the members, the grounds crew, all the employees, knew him and were fond of him. We would drive around the golf course in the evening as a family, checking on the conditions, and people always seemed happy to see us."

His dad wasn't the only person Matt liked to help. "He was the kind of kid who would do the right thing even if nobody was looking," explains Jackie. "He was so different than a typical teenage boy. Limited interest in video games, loved school, loved to do his homework, couldn't wait to get to the golf course, either to play, practice or work with his dad. He went out of his way to help me, his brothers, grandparents, his friends. He was a treasure, an old soul."

Jackie and Dave immediately threw all their energy into Matt's treatments, relying on friends and family to assist with Matt's twin brother Tommy, and younger brother Andrew. He missed six months of eighth grade year in treatment at the Children's Hospital of Philadelphia, all the while as concerned with his family as he was with himself. States Jackie, "he would get out of a difficult or painful treatment, chemo or something like it, and immediately worry about me. 'Mom, are you OK?' He was more concerned with my emotional wellbeing than his own physical state. He was a remarkable kid."

While in remission, Matt returned to the golf course, the place he loved best, often accompanied by his mother. Jackie had slowly become enamored of the game, finding time despite the demands of her career in the dental field and attention to her three sons. "I had been around the game for so long through my husband, and thought playing with Matt would be an unusual mother-son bonding experience. So I took it up, and really enjoyed it." The tumor's location affected Matt's balance and swing, and both his fine and gross motor skills. His golf game never fully recovered, but thanks to speech and occupational therapy, other than a slight left hand tremor he was almost his former self.

Though he fought his illness bravely, Matt passed in late summer 2010, about two years after his initial diagnosis, shortly before his freshman year of high school. Dave and Jackie initiated the Matthew Renk Foundation shortly thereafter to honor their son's memory. The foundation exists to help children suffering with brain cancer and their families. The funds distributed can help with medical treatment, for gas money or other transportation costs, for special furniture either in the hospital room or back at home, for funeral expenses, even to buy gifts or toys for the patient's siblings who get so much less of their parent's attention when their brother or sister becomes gravely ill. States Jackie, "Our primary goal is to help families and patients get through the emotional and financial challenges associated with brain cancer."

The membership and board of Lookaway Golf Club, as it had done so often during Matt's long illness, stepped to the plate

and began hosting a golf event to raise funds for the foundation. It was, and remains, the only charity outing on the club's yearly calendar, and virtually all the participants are club members. "It's astounding to us that the membership is willing to pay thousands of dollars for the privilege of playing their own course to support this cause," states Dave Renk, with a sense of wonder. "We thought it might peter out after a year or two, but instead the tournament is becoming more popular with each passing year."

"The impact that the Renk family has had on Lookaway is immeasurable," begins club General Manager John Pitocchelli. "The entire family has grown up around the course, and Dave Renk takes extreme pride and ownership in creating a special experience here. Matt was positioning himself as his dad's successor and might have taken over when Dave retired. The membership truly values the impact the Renk Family has had on making this such a golf haven, and their ongoing generosity is a testament to this fine young man taken from us way too early."

One of the foundation's favored projects is helping with the construction costs of the respite garden at the Children's Hospital of Philadelphia, which is where Matt spent months on end during his treatment. "The hospital is outstanding, and the quality of care from the nurses, doctors, surgeons and support staff there was wonderful," relates Jackie Renk, "They made our son as comfortable as possible under the circumstances. But its location in Center City is truly the concrete jungle, nothing but buildings in every direction, with no green space. The respite garden is being constructed to allow patients and their families to enjoy some greenery, some plant life and a feeling of being outdoors while taking treatment in the middle of a major city."

"We were very lucky with our support system," states Dave. The club and its membership were amazing, and it's basically the same board of governors now as was there when I was hired in the late 90s. It's a tremendous testament that they continue to stand by our family and remember Matt by staging our golf tournament year after year."

What a lovely, albeit bittersweet irony. The Renk Family was embraced and supported through the entire nightmarish ordeal of Matthew's illness, treatment and eventual passing by the members and employees of the posh and exclusive Lookaway Golf Club. For two years time, these busy and successful members helped take on the incredible burden facing Dave and Jackie. Now they offer ongoing support by patronizing their tournament. Though it is their prerogative to do so, virtually none choose to look away.

For more information visit: www.matthewrenkfoundation.org

The Maui Jim Golf Classic

"Aloha." It's not the typical greeting you expect to hear in Peoria, Illinois. This is the heart of the heartland, not a palm tree on the landscape, a thousand miles from the nearest ocean, where temperatures hover near freezing for months at a stretch.

However, "aloha" is more than just a Hawaiian greeting. In the native language it means affection, peace, compassion, and mercy. These are the qualities espoused by the management team at Maui Jim, a high-end sunglasses and optical company that is improbably headquartered in Peoria, a somewhat downtrodden blue-collar city of 115,000 hardworking souls. They devote much of their benevolence to the Children's Home Association of Illinois, helping to improve the lives of thousands of kids who've been dealt a tough hand. Whether it's missing, neglectful or abusive parents, aberrant social behavior, psychological issues, or criminal activities initiated by parent or child, the fact is there are some twenty thousand wards of the state in Illinois. The Children's Home Association tries to help every kid it can, and they are grateful for the help offered to their organization by Maui Jim.

Mike Dalton is the president of the company, and has been at the helm since 1996. He was working in the optical business in Peoria at the time, and when offered the job heading up Maui Jim, decided to expand on his existing base of employees, infrastructure and warehousing, and to take advantage of his centralized Midwest location.

His affinity for the Children's Home Association of Illinois is easy to understand: his own father was an orphan. "During World War II my dad and his sisters lost their parents," begins Dalton, who oversees five hundred employees

at their Peoria base, and hundreds of others in locations as diverse as Australia, Mexico, Canada, Hawaii, France, Germany and India. "Dad ended up on a work farm for several years, where he survived by occasionally resorting to pig slop for sustenance. He ran away several times, ending up at an orphanage. They were able to place him with distant relatives in British Columbia, though he lost track of his sisters for twenty years."

Dalton's dad recovered from his traumatic childhood, becoming a commander in the Canadian Navy and a father of six. His son always credits the orphanage with saving him. "If he hadn't landed there, who knows what might have happened to him?"

Matt George serves as the CEO of the Children's Home Association of Illinois, and wonders about the fate of his youthful charges on a daily basis. "We are heavily state-funded, and in this time of government cutbacks we are extremely fortunate to have Maui Jim help us provide the necessary programs for the kids in our community."

The non-profit's CEO has a famous first cousin in former

National Football League quarterback Jeff George, the first pick in the 1990 draft who ended up playing for six teams over more than a dozen seasons. "I ran the Jeff George Foundation for years, and we had fundraising events all over the country, wherever my cousin was playing at that time," continues Matt George, who now is responsible for an annual budget of $25,000,000, and 450 employees. "I can tell you that no matter how many NFL players were in attendance, no matter how upscale or glitzy any event might be, it wasn't better, more memorable than what we have in Peoria with the Maui Jim Golf Classic. Nor have I been around any event that consistently raises as much money."

If you want a lei to be placed over your floral print shirt by a grass-skirt-wearing hula girl, options around Peoria are limited. Best bet? Take part in the Maui Jim Golf Classic, which features a poolside luau the evening before the tournament. "The aloha spirit goes beyond our annual golf event," continues Mike Dalton. "We try and live it every day as a company, and assist the young people who need our help the most in the city where we choose to headquarter our company."

"Aloha philosophy teaches us that we are all connected, and only as strong as the weakest link," continues the company president. "There's nobody weaker in our area than these kids, and it's our mission to assist them." More than $300,000 is raised yearly at their golf event, and the company makes a habit of hiring kids who've come through the Children's Home Association system. "They start on a six month probationary period, and if all works out, they come on full time."

Residential, transitional, and independent living are three of the ways the Children's Home Association takes care of displaced youth. They also offer foster care services and run three schools. One of the schools is for those on the autism spectrum and another is called Youth Farm, where troubled kids live "without bars on the windows," according to Matt George.

Regarding the housing element, George continues, "We help younger kids by keeping them in house, offering counseling, and getting them to school. Eventually they transition to being somewhat independent, and need to be able to find and keep a job, navigate the city with bus passes, et cetera. Eventually, if they are still in the system, they live in small groups independently, with an adult coordinator who takes on the role of a fraternity mom or a resident assistant. We hope to turn all kids into productive, tax-paying, gainfully employed citizens."

A shocking statistic: the average age of a homeless person in Peoria is nine. While there are plenty of adult homeless, the average age is skewed so low because so many homeless are young teens with several babies or toddlers. However, not every kid in the system is a hard case. "We had one teenage boy who was arrested more than twenty times," recalls George. "But virtually all of those arrests were for stealing food for his younger siblings. It's gratifying to know that Mike Dalton and his staff have a passion for helping out kids who are or have been behind the eight-ball, it comes from the heart, from the aloha spirit."

At Maui Jim, "aloha" is not just a buzzword or catchphrase. Concludes Dalton, "We talk about it at every company gathering. It means giving of yourself without expecting anything in return. It means coordinating your mind and heart so you're always emitting good feelings towards others. It's a business philosophy as well as a personal one. There's no unimportant job at this company, everyone has to do what's required of them to make things work right. By the same token, there are no unimportant people in the world."

It's heartwarming to know that a company that manufactures a luxury item like high-end sunglasses, sold across the globe, would be so committed to helping out the indigent, unfortunate and disaffected youth found in their hardscrabble hometown.

For more information visit: www.chail.org

Mighty Oakes Heart Foundation Golf Tournament

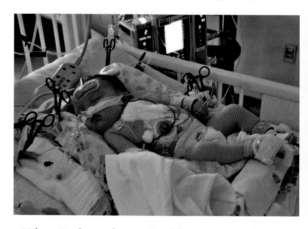

When Becky and Greg Ortyl (pronounced "or-tell") went to the obstetrician's office for an ultrasound midway through her second pregnancy, the only surprise they anticipated was the gender of their coming baby. Instead they were blindsided by the news that their unborn child had a congenital heart defect. Of all the roller coaster moments and hairpin turns that defined their lives for nearly two more years, none hit as hard as that initial news. Begins Becky, "It was a bombshell, and took us totally aback. I don't know how we drove home, the day was such a blur as we came to grips with our new reality."

The baby had been diagnosed with truncus arteriosus, and would need major surgery within a few days of birth, followed by a second procedure as a toddler, and a third near puberty. His parents were reassured that while it's a rare and severe surgery, barring complications, the afflicted child will lead a rich, full life. Their hopes were further buoyed by the fact that one of the nation's leading surgical specialists was right there in St. Louis.

"We had to redesign our hopes and dreams for our son, though we still foresaw a future where he played high school baseball like his dad, went on family vacations with his big sister Isla, a full life. We figured he'd be a kid with a scar on his chest, no big

deal," continues Becky.

The only thing riskier than major surgery on a newborn was major surgery on a premature one. So Becky's doctors insisted she avoid travel, stress, and almost all activity to ensure the baby would come to full term.

It was unrealistic advice, considering the gravity of the situation and the fact that daughter Isla was a typically active toddler at that time. "Greg and I spent the remainder of the pregnancy reassuring each other we could handle what was coming. We were all holding our breath together."

Their son Oakes was born in March of 2011. Despite the months of trepidation leading up to that day, the Ortyls were lucky that his heart defect had been diagnosed in advance, as many aren't. There was a complete medical team at the ready, nearly twenty in all. Shortly after an uneventful birth, the baby Oakes, full-sized, pink, and ogled by his parents and all in attendance, was whisked to the neonatal intensive care unit at the children's hospital. "If a heart defect isn't discovered beforehand, the baby can quickly go into distress, need emergency care, sometimes requiring a life-flight helicopter to the appropriate hospital. So we were fortu-

nate that the entire team was ready when the baby came," continues Greg.

When Oakes went in for heart surgery five days after birth, it was discovered he had a malformed trachea. Consequently, the operation was delayed for nearly a week, as they waited for the proper specialist to become available. "Our son was fine," recalls Becky. He looked good, was eating and sleeping with no distress. But my intuition also told me that this tracheal problem was the harbinger of other complications to follow." If only she had been wrong.

Oakes recovered well enough after the initial procedures to finally come home, around Memorial Day, when he was little more than two months old. Sadly, the two weeks he spent at home with his family would be the only time he ever left the hospital.

"He didn't look right to me, and was acting sluggishly, so I rushed him to the doctor's," recalls a sighing Becky. "His heart rate and blood pressure were so high that initially the nurse thought the

monitoring machines were malfunctioning and giving faulty readings." Oakes needed emergency surgery again, to replace faulty heart valves that were inserted during his first procedure. Once again he recovered. "Everyone around him referred to him as a badass," states his dad. "He kept bouncing back from these major events, and would be smiling, serene, sucking his thumb. All the doctors and nurses were amazed at his resilience."

By July, more bad news was in the offing. It was discovered that Oakes had pulmonary vein stenosis, which is the narrowing of the veins from the heart to the lungs. It necessitates a lung transplant, a brutal procedure for any being, never mind one as vulnerable as a four-month old baby.

As they considered this drastic surgery, a hospital counselor was at once pitiless and pragmatic, stating, "it's not a matter of if, but when you will bury your son." She recommended palliative care for Oakes, letting nature take its course and keeping him comfortable in his final days. But ultimately they decided to fight for their baby, the same

way he had been fighting every day since birth. The lung transplant followed, and while that was the last of the surgeries, the year that followed was filled with chemotherapy, pheresis, dialysis, transfusions, catheterizations and stents. The doctors were using every means possible to keep Oakes from rejecting the transplanted lungs.

Though he fought bravely, Oakes finally started to succumb to his physical frailties the following summer. "We had hoped to take our 'miracle child' home again, but he faltered, and the doctors told us there was nothing more to be done," recounts Becky, in wavering voice.

On the day that Becky and Greg withdrew care, letting their son go, they were far from alone. The room was filled with all the doctors, nurses and medical professionals who had cared for Oakes and were emotionally invested in his battle through all those turbulent times. Amidst all the heartbreak and the raw emotion of the day, there was a sense of incredulity at how long and hard that "badass" baby fought. A quiet pulmonologist offered the opinion that Oakes had battled so valiantly because he wanted to be with and stay with his family, who loved him so much, and were pulling for him as hard as was humanly possible.

Despite all their travails, the Ortyls felt they were fortunate to be in their own home, surrounded by family and friends, with expert medical care at St. Louis Children's Hospital. They realized that other families around the nation had to endure

the same stress and uncertainty, but often do so far from home. That's what compelled them to form the Mighty Oakes Heart Foundation, which provides financial support to families coping with the traumatic reality of congenital heart defects, the nation's most common birth defect. More than $600,000 has been raised since Oakes' passing, much of that sum due to the golf tournament that was initiated in 2013. "We'll make mortgage payments for parents who cannot leave their child's bedside to work, cover rent or utilities, help them pay for a temporary apartment in the city where they've relocated for medical care, whatever's needed," states Greg. "We've never turned down a dire or legitimate request for financial assistance, and as long as we have the means to do so, we never will."

Mighty oaks are among the most impressive species in the forest. These trees can live for over two hundred years, and as they do their roots entangle, and their branches can intertwine or grow straight to the heavens. Baby Oakes was here and gone in a relative instant, just sixteen months, all but a few precious weeks spent hospitalized. His roots never really had the chance to take hold, though his brief life intertwined with so many others: family, friends, caring medical professionals, who knew and loved him. He went straight towards the heavens himself, leaving behind not only his grieving family but also the Mighty Oakes Heart Foundation. Like the majestic hardwood itself, it will endure beyond our lifetimes.

For more information visit: www.mightyoakes.org

The Mission YMCA Pro-Am

San Francisco has recently usurped New York as the nation's most expensive city. Not hard to fathom, considering the proliferation of tech moguls, venture capitalists and Silicon Valley wizards who call the Bay Area home.

Despite the prevalence of wealth, the city has its middle class and underclass, and the various YMCAs, which have been serving San Francisco for 160 years, are scattered through town to help serve these populations. None are more in need than the Mission Y, serving the population of mostly blue-collar neighborhoods like the Mission, Excelsior, Glen Park, Bernal Heights, Visitacion Valley and Potrero Hill.

The Mission Y boasts a fine playground, serviceable meeting rooms and a popular culinary program aimed at budding teenage chefs. They also offer a pre-school, a community garden, teen and senior programs, and partner with area schools to provide on-site childcare for working people in the neighborhood. With so much going on and few avenues for generating income, it relies on the YMCA board for much of its operating revenue. Luckily a dedicated group of area professionals add a much needed revenue stream by virtue of their long-running, highly popular golf outing.

"One day I was on the phone, the next day I was on the letterhead!" So begins the congenial Walker Bass, an executive with a "Big Four" accounting firm, who quite by happenstance took a leadership position with the tournament more than a decade ago. He, like virtually all of his equally long-serving colleagues on their

the **Y** **19th Annual YMCA Pro-Am**
Mercedes-Benz Dealer Championships Benefiting the Mission Y

grassroots committee, has zero regrets.

"The Mission District is historically a lower-income neighborhood, with a majority Latino and African-American population," explains Hank Bannister, who spent many years as the tournament's chairman before relinquishing the reins. "We are big believers in community outreach, and our annual tournament is a great way to give back to a neighborhood in need. We all have grown to love and embrace the event."

It's certainly easy to embrace the exquisite golf course on which the tournament is contested. About an hour south of the city in Santa Cruz lies Pasatiempo, an Alister MacKenzie masterpiece dating from 1929 that is one of the truly great semi-private facilities in the West. The view of the course from the winding driveway as one climbs towards the clubhouse reveals some of the most elegant and distinctive bunkering found anywhere in the nation. The course is rugged but walker-friendly, with significant elevation changes, plenty of natural hazards and excruciatingly difficult greens.

"It's ironic that the Mission Y is housed in a low-slung, non-descript building, one you wouldn't necessarily notice as you walked past," offers tournament co-chairman Brian Hetherington, thoughtfully. "But we hold its benefit tournament at this amazingly memorable location, a golf venue that everyone knows, loves, and cannot wait to play each year. In certain ways it's the key ingredient to our success."

Also key to the event's success is Pasatiempo's longtime head professional Ken Woods, who has heartily welcomed the event practically from the outset. "The Mission Y Event has played a huge part in our golf club's recent history," offers Woods. "Since its inception in 1997, I've had the privilege and honor to be a part of fifteen of them. Knowing that my role in organizing a portion of the event that has raised over a million dollars for underprivileged kids is more gratifying than words can say."

Adds Hetherington, "Ken Woods is a real gem, a wonderful guy, but he shows his diabolical side the day of the event.

You cannot believe how fast he gets the greens rolling, or the evil places he puts the pin!"

While the tournament celebrates its twentieth anniversary in 2016, another key Mission Y fundraiser, an epicurean evening of fine food and wine, is of more recent vintage. "When our golf revenues started tailing off during the financial crisis in 2008 and beyond, we realized we needed an added spark to keep the money flowing to our Y," relates Hetherington, an insurance executive. "So our same committee concocted an evening we call 'Sip and Savor,' sponsored by an area Mercedes-Benz dealership, which has taken on a life of its own."

The beauty of the evening is that the gourmands aren't necessarily golfers, and vice-versa. "Our golf tournament is robust once again," continues Bass. "But our wine and food gala, which takes place in springtime, attracts a different crowd entirely. Between the two events we are proud to be raising six figures annually for our Y." One can imagine the quality of libations, culled from the award-winning

wineries of nearby Napa, alongside the culinary genius of some of San Francisco's most innovative chefs. But all that said, the summertime Pro-Am at beloved "Pasa" doesn't take a back seat.

The event features four amateurs and an area pro, and woe to the group's scorekeeper who gets caught up in the sweeping golf course views, because there's plenty to keep track of. "The area professionals are playing for a significant cash purse of their own," explains Hetherington. "The team event features two best balls out of five, with or without the pro's assistance. And there are also individual prizes for low gross and low net among the amateurs. So all told there are three tournaments happening concurrently."

The pros show their worth not only on the course, but also at the silent auction during the post-tournament party. They offer up coveted experiences like complimentary twosomes or foursomes, playing lessons, perhaps lunch and a round of golf at their respective clubs. And with a murderer's row of private clubs in the

area represented by these professionals, Olympic Club, San Francisco Golf Club and the California Golf Club of San Francisco, to name but three, bidding is spirited and uninhibited, to say the least.

Concludes Walker Bass, "This event has become an important part of our lives, and supporting it enthusiastically is something we take real pride in. Our tournament, usually scheduled for a Thursday in mid-August, has always been great fun. Truth be told, it is pretty much my favorite day of the year!"

For more information
visit: www.ymcaproam.org

The Mississippi Children's Hospital Pro-Am

Friends of CHILDREN'S HOSPITAL

The Batson Children's Hospital in the capital of Jackson, Mississippi fights an uphill battle. In a state famous for the Delta blues, endless fields of cotton, and its eponymous river, the health concerns of the citizenry are notorious. By many objective measures, the Magnolia State ranks dead last in terms of major health grades, with disproportionately high incidences of obesity, hypertension, diabetes and infant mortality rates.

The dedicated medical staff at the state's only children's hospital works tirelessly to ensure that its youngest citizens receive the best care possible, encouraging them to buck the trend plaguing many of their elders, so that they might grow up leading healthier lives.

The hospital prides itself on taking care of all children – those with private insurance, those on Medicaid, and those who have no money at all. Located on the campus of the University of Mississippi Medical Center, the 225-bed Batson Children's Hospital has 140 pediatric specialists on staff. Many of these doctors are fanned out across the state, working at satellite clinics in Gulfport, Hattiesburg and Tupelo. Dr. Robert Abney, a native Mississippian who began his practice as both a pediatrician and pediatric cardiologist in1969, admits, "though our adult population has health challenges, our youngsters are resilient, and don't have ingrained lifetime habits. Many are healthy and active, and we are proud to have one of the nation's highest immunization rates for young children."

Mississippi's Children's Hospital Pro-Am is one of the marquee events staged by Friends of Children's Hospital, which is the health care facility's charitable arm. Dr. Abney has been intimately involved since the tournament's first days, nearly a quarter century past. He explains that "At the beginning we invited LPGA players to take part in the event, trying to differentiate ourselves from the 'disease of the week' golf tournaments that are so common nationwide. However their travel costs and related expenses ate into our profits so much we were barely breaking even, so we changed tactics." Abney and his co-founder, Jackson-area businessman Sidney Allen, started bringing in club professionals from around the Gulf States region to play with the paying customers, and the concept was a hit. "We were helped by the Gulf States PGA Section, who helped us cultivate a number of club professionals from around the region, which was mutually beneficial. These pros get to meet and mingle with many of Jackson's business elite, while our players get to meet and play with pros from all over the area."

The tournament expanded from a single course in Jackson to the 36-hole Dancing Rabbit complex up the road some eighty miles in the town of Philadelphia. But after a few years hosting this "away game," the organizers came to understand that the vast majority of funds were still emanating from Jackson, so for convenience sake they returned to the original host venue, the highly regarded Annandale Golf Club, then expanding to a second course and eventually a third. Logistics were helped by the fact that these other host venues, Reunion Golf and Country Club and The Country Club of Jackson, were in close proximity to Annandale.

One of the main challenges, and among the primary goals of its signature golf tournament is erasing the "out of sight, out of mind" mentality that the hospital battles. "Of course, we are trying to raise money," explains Melanie Schade, who serves as tournament coordinator, among other roles at Friends of Children's Hospital. "Since we've expanded to three courses and host nearly four hundred players we are generally adding between $80,000 and $110,000 to our coffers each year. We've raised in excess of a million dollars in the last decade alone. But equally important is raising our profile. So doctors in rural areas, or parents of ill children far from Jackson, realize there's a world-class facility to treat their children within the state borders, no need to fly to a large city, or travel out-of-state."

The golf tournament, known as the Trustmark Children's Hospital Pro-Am, draws the vast majority of its support from the greater Jackson region, both in participants and sponsorship dollars. "As we recruit teams from further afield to play in the event, it also helps bring awareness of the hospital to these areas," continues Schade. "Because the golf pros arrive from all over the region they help us get the word out, but we want more of the paying participants to come from other areas of Mississippi, so their awareness of who we are and what we do can grow."

"Our challenge is not getting the word out about our hospital here in Jackson, where we are well known, but getting the word out elsewhere, so parents and grandparents think of us first should their youngsters encounter a major health concern," relates Abney.

The tournament principals emphasize the event runs lean and mean. "Most charitable entities are pleased if they can limit administrative costs to twenty percent," explains Abney. "With our forty-five-plus volunteer board, made up largely of doctors, administrators and community leaders, with only two paid employees, we limit our costs to just five percent. We also feel it's imperative to keep our prices reasonable. We could charge more to play and make more for the hospital, but want

to keep our event affordable for the community at large."

Adds Schade, "The proceeds from our tournament benefits the Child Life Program. We strive to make long hospital stays more pleasant and normal for the kids, and therefore provide art therapy, pet therapy, music therapy, and other recreational and educational opportunities to keep their spirits buoyed."

Abney now serves as a professor emeritus at the hospital, and is quick to give credit to three key sponsors of the long running event. "If not for the ongoing support of Trustmark National Bank, Mercedes-Benz of Jackson and First Choice Medical, we would not have enjoyed the success we have today."

"Outside event coordinators have approached us repeatedly to take over the event," states Abney. "Understandable, considering its size and scope, and the high profile it has within our state. But we've resisted all these requests. We desire to run it ourselves, it's a passion for our whole group, and we prefer to keep the money in house, and not give away a percentage to a management group." Concludes Schade, "every dollar we don't spend is one more dollar we can use at our hospital, to benefit the children."

**For more
information visit: www.foch.org**

The National Capital Golf Classic

NATIONAL CAPITAL GOLF CLASSIC

AN AMERICAN CANCER SOCIETY EVENT

It's not that Mark Larsen doesn't believe in doctors. It's just that he doesn't believe everything they tell him.

His proactive behavior with a series of medical professionals helped save his life. A survivor of prostate cancer for some two decades, Larsen was a staunch advocate for his own health. For nearly twenty years the mega-successful charity golf tournament he founded has been raising significant money, but more importantly, it pounds home the same simple message to all of its attendees: get checked, ask questions, be aggressive and not passive when it comes to matters of your own health.

His parents' premature deaths from cancer (in their mid fifties, barely a year apart) heightened Larsen's sensitivity to his own health. "My mom died first, of abdominal cancer, I always felt my dad died as much from a broken heart as from colon cancer," begins Larsen, who makes his home in northern Virginia.

In his mid twenties, the commercial real estate broker found an aggressive doctor willing to treat him like he was fifteen years older. He subsequently got involved with the American Cancer Society, helping to run a few programs in his area. He met his future wife, Cindy, around this time. Eerily, she had lost her fiancée to a car crash less than two months before, within a day or so of Larsen's father's passing. "Our happenstance meeting was the silver lining among the dark clouds," offers Cindy. "We were married about three years later."

Because of his genetics, Larsen insisted on regular colonoscopies as he moved towards his thirties, decades before most doctors deem them necessary. When his preferred doctor stopped taking insurance, he changed practitioners. His new MD felt an irregularity in his prostate and ordered the PSA (Prostate Specific Antigen) test.

A week later the results were back with Larsen's being, as the doctor put it "a little high for a thirty-eight year old but a little low for a forty-two year old." Then he recommended "watchful waiting."

"To me, the concept of watchful waiting meant waiting for a potential cancer to get worse, courting sickness or even death," continues Larsen, who insisted on a biopsy, and went to a urologist to get one. The urologist also counselled that insurance was not likely to pay for a biopsy, but Larsen again pushed through and said if need be he would pay for the test. When the ensuing results confirmed his fears, showing prostate cancer, he was steered by his medical professionals towards Patrick Walsh at Johns Hopkins University in Baltimore, considered by his peers to be "the Michael Jordan" of prostate cancer surgery. Walsh invented all of the modern methods for treatment of this type of cancer and contributed greatly to the discovery of the PSA blood antigen method of uncovering this cancer.

In another unfortunate and peculiar coincidence, the day after Larsen got his diagnosis, Cindy miscarried their third child. "Despite all this upheaval, we went ahead with a scheduled vacation to Disney World with our two young kids. That's when I was called and told I could get into see Dr. Walsh within a few weeks, when normally the lead time for an appointment is several months."

On the initial visit to his office, Walsh, a pioneer in various advanced surgical techniques and a respected teacher, researcher, and surgeon, explained why he made room on his calendar. "He told me that despite the rigor of his daily schedule,

if he has the chance to add decades to a young man's life, particularly a father with young children, that would be a priority," recalls Larsen, who underwent surgery several weeks later on his thirty-ninth birthday.

After six weeks of recuperation with no activity, Larsen ventured to a school fundraiser for one of his children. He recounted his medical ordeal to a friend named Frank MacDonell, who soon after suggested they start a golf event for prostate cancer, not just to raise funds, but also awareness. "Studies show that most men over fifty have developed some degree of prostate cancer already," explains Larsen, now some twenty years past those severe health troubles. "If it stays encapsulated in the prostate it's far less lethal then if it ends up spreading to the pelvic bones, spine, and other organs. Then it becomes a fast-moving, hard-to-treat cancer that potentially becomes deadly."

Their original goal was modest: attempt to raise five thousand dollars and increase awareness. Now there have been about twenty iterations of the annual event, and

millions raised for the American Cancer Society. How to explain the longevity and success?

"Part of it is that prostate cancer events are somewhat rare," continues Larsen, who stepped down as chairman after more than fifteen years at the helm. "Another reason is that we seek out marketing dollars as opposed to charitable dollars." He differentiates the two by saying that by putting on a top-notch event at high-end venues (the tournament has been held at the Robert Trent Jones Golf Club, Woodmont Country Club and Trump National DC, among others) and omitting mulligans, auctions, raffle tickets, etc., the attendees can just focus on a good time without being asked to reach into their pocket for these extras. The event attracts serious golfers, playing their own ball, as opposed to the typical scramble or captain's choice format. "We tend to attract a high-level field of participants who want to support our cause, but also see the advantage of hosting their integral employees or customers out for the day. It's slightly different mindset than getting a field whose sole focus is just the charity. The clients have a wonderful day and leave with a number of high end gifts too!"

Jeremy Bardin is an area construction executive and the event's current chairman. "We attract many of the area's industry leaders in the real estate, banking, automobile and commercial management markets. The Board is very careful about maximizing the player experience, as we know that a day off from work (on the Monday following Father's Day) is tough to come by for many business leaders. It's our goal to ensure that the experience of participating in our tournament is as recognizably great every year as it was when I first attended more than a decade ago."

The tournament committee is vital to this event. It is mostly comprised of well-connected business owners and influential professionals in the area. They leverage their relationships amongst vendors, suppliers, employees, colleagues and other associates to ensure a full-field turnout every year. They also use their acumen and the American Cancer Society's good name to negotiate the best price on all goods and services associated with the tournament, so there's more money going to prostate cancer research.

The event has raised in excess of four million dollars, but what gives the founder just as much satisfaction is changing the mindset of his attendees. Concludes Larsen, "What I love most of all is hearing from someone who attended the tournament, which prompted them to get checked. They often receive a clean bill of health, or they might get diagnosed early, and get things under control. I sincerely believe that we have contributed top saving the lives of fathers, brothers, sons and husbands! Stories telling of this are the most gratifying thing of all."

Happily, Larsen acted similarly all those years ago, allowing him to keep telling his story, one golfer at a time.

For more information
visit: www.nationalcapitalgolfclassic.org

The Northeast Arc Commodore Invitational

We live in politically correct times, which is in many ways a good thing. The fact is that upon its founding in the mid 50s, the 'Arc' designation in Northeast Arc was meant as an acronym for the Association of Retarded Children. But over the decades, the organization has expanded its scope and become more broadly based, growing to encompass a wider range of the citizenry, well beyond those with just developmental disabilities. Though not part of their official mandate, it's easy to surmise that the 'Arc' portion of their name relates to the arc of life, as they provide support and assistance from infanthood to old age. "We assist those with autism, intellectual disabilities, deafness, physical challenges, traumatic brain injuries, and myriad other difficulties," explains CEO Jerry McCarthy.

"We help more than a hundred individuals with housing needs alone," explains the CEO, who began his career with the organization, which is based in greater Boston, in 1979. "In extreme cases they might be on ventilators, in wheelchairs, and need twenty-four-hour care. On the other end of the spectrum we assist those who are fully functional, but might need an assist with banking or negotiating a lease."

"Family support services are key elements," continues McCarthy. "We help those caring for family members with relief, training or counseling, so they can keep their loved ones at home. We also offer occupational and vocational training, provide support staff to help new employees at a company ease into their duties in a non-stressful way. We even offer comprehensive job placement."

In short, this amazing organization provides all manner of programs, mentorship and support for a huge population of people with disabilities. It is a special organization, as is the one-of-a-kind venue where they gather for their annual charity golf tournament.

The back story: Michael Frangos was for many years a prominent restaurateur in suburban Beverly, Massachusetts, some twenty-five miles north of Boston. The Commodore was a well-known, lively and successful eatery for decades, and when the owner, who had a brother with developmental disabilities, decided to initiate a golf tournament to raise funds for the Northeast Arc, the name was self-evident.

The Commodore Invitational Golf Tournament debuted in 1970, and for a quarter century was held at a 'gourmet's choice' of the most coveted private clubs on Boston's scenic North Shore. It touched down at Salem Country Club, Tedesco, Essex County Club and Kernwood, among others. But for more than a dozen years it has been ensconced at what many believe to be the crown jewel of the region. The tournament has found a permanent home at the whimsically named, quirkily rumpled, and fescue-framed Myopia Hunt Club. Myopia, which hosted the U.S. Open for the fourth and final time in 1908, is one of the most historically significant, not to mention one of the most beguilingly beautiful and fun-to-play golf courses in the nation. It also serves as a financial juggernaut for the Northeast Arc, one of the most vital annual fundraisers they host.

"I wanted to leverage my many business and banking contacts in Boston to support the Northeast Arc in an enthusiastic and meaningful way," begins current tournament chairman Mark Thompson, the CEO and president of Boston Private Bank and Trust Company. "So many North Shore courses are exceptional. But Myopia has the 'wow' factor, the cachet, the once-a-

year-treat mentality that will compel busy executives with numerous responsibilities to get out of the city, take the drive up and enjoy the day. This way we get them involved, eager, and hopefully donating significantly to this broad-based organization that positively affects the lives of many thousands who need support."

Thompson, who also serves as Chairman of the Northeast Arc Advisory Board, is a case in point. When he took over the chairmanship of The Commodore in 1994, his bank was stretching to make a modest five-figure donation to his local Arc. Over the decades, as his business flourished and expanded, so did his financial commitment and personal investment in the cause. "This is one of the top five Arc chapters in the nation, helping more than seven thousand individuals in 150 different cities and towns, with an annual budget of $170 million. It's a fantastic cause, and we are so proud of our long association," continues the native Bostonian.

"We wholeheartedly support the efforts they make to assist so many challenged individuals, who might otherwise be marginalized by society. They become active, vibrant, vital members of their communities. These are intensely loyal, diligent and hard-working people. In this day and age finding hourly wage workers invested in their job is no easy task. But those of us who take the time to know them and be around them realize they are a credit to themselves, their employers, and the businesses they work for."

The longevity in chairing the Commodore between founder Frangos and successor Thompson for more than forty-five years brings to mind the half-century of service by a trio of Red Sox left-fielders, plying their trade in the shadow of the iconic Green Monster at Boston's historic Fenway Park. Ted Williams, Carl Yastrzemski and Jim Rice were the three sentinels on duty between 1939 and 1989. All ended up in the Hall of Fame. Frangos and Thompson, while less celebrated, are equally admired for their dedication to the cause.

Commenting on the fact that tournament's annual revenue has grown tenfold from about twenty thousand dollars to more than $200,000 since he took over in the mid-90s, Thompson offers the following: "I think society at large has gotten more comfortable with those who have disabilities, it isn't the 'dark secret' mentality that existed decades past. That's why we have the type of widespread support that was harder to find in the early years. That, and the fact that Myopia is such a marquee, must-visit venue, and we make a point of going back there every year."

Just a fraction of the Northeast Arc's five hundred full-time employees, one hundred part-time employees, and seven hundred volunteers have ever taken the step back in time that is a day at the delightfully antiquated Myopia Hunt Club. But it doesn't faze them, because these dedicated men and women are more concerned with helping those in their charge attend public schools, develop friendships, reside in the neighborhoods of their choice and earn a paycheck. Their impetus is helping those in need to live their lives to the fullest, from the cradle to the grave.

For more information visit: www.ne-arc.org

The Parkinson Council Golf Classic

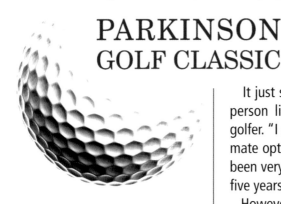

PARKINSON
GOLF CLASSIC

It just so happens that the world's most famous person living with Parkinson's disease is also a golfer. "I started golf in my forties, which is the ultimate optimism," recounts Michael J. Fox, who has been very much in the public eye for the last thirty-five years on television and in film.

However, there was far less optimism some years back when Philadelphian Jan Albert and the Parkinson Council was approached about starting a golf tournament to raise funds to combat the disease that afflicted her mother. Ironic, as Albert was an avid golfer herself.

"I thought the market for charity tournaments was oversaturated, and we would be hard pressed to find players," begins the longtime member of the Parkinson Council in Philadelphia. "Turns out I was dead wrong."

"We were approached by a young man named David Halpern, an avid golfer whose dad, a noted surgeon, had Parkinson's. We were skeptical, but David wouldn't be dissuaded, so we gave it a shot."

You couldn't have blamed them for throwing in the towel, which happened to be soaking wet, after their initial effort. It stormed so violently on the inaugural date, slated for the classic Huntingdon Valley Country Club, that the event was postponed for months and finally rescheduled at the Philadelphia Country Club. Fortunately, one of the city's great gifts to the wider world (along with cheesesteaks and Rocky Balboa) is its abundance of magnificent golf venues, and over the years as the event has gained both momentum and wider awareness, the Parkinson Council Golf Classic has done the grand tour.

It wasn't long before they needed thirty-six holes to handle the surfeit of avid patrons they were at-

tracting. In the early years they visited Aronimink and Green Valley in addition to the aforementioned Philadelphia Country Club. After the tournament grew into something those clubs could not accommodate, they moved to venerable multi-course venues such as Philadelphia Cricket Club, Saucon Valley, and Philmont. But while the locations varied, the tournament vibe has never wavered.

"I've played in many charity events over the years," relates Albert, who over time has served as the event's chairman, honoree, and for many years as honorary chairman. "One of the reasons we have this loyal clientele is our extremely enthusiastic group of volunteers who return yearly. They all are touched by the disease in some way, as so many people are. They are gregarious, great cheerleaders, tend to dress similarly, and add zest to the event, at registration, on the par-three holes, and throughout the day. It's almost as though each group has their own gallery of fans as they come through."

The tournament has come through with more than three and a half million dollars for local programs, research and services to combat Parkinson's over its more than fifteen-year history. Like all long-running charity events, the Parkinson Council Golf Classic

has endured ebbs and flows over the years, with more or fewer dollars raised depending on that year's honoree, timing, weather, venue, turnout, etc.

At a recent nadir there was talk of winding this tournament down for good, but a fortunate-yet-unfortunate twist of fate intervened. "A dynamic fellow named Ken Gilberg volunteered as chairman," relates Albert. "His wife has Parkinson's, so he was raring to go, wanting to keep our event vital, which is great. However in the big picture the fact that there is constantly 'new blood' like Ken means that the fight to cure this disease remains an uphill battle."

"With Parkinson's, it's like you're in the middle of the street and you're stuck there in cement shoes and you know a bus is coming at you, but you don't know when," continues a thoughtful Michael J. Fox. "You think you can hear it rumbling, but you have a lot of time to think. When I first publicly acknowledged my diagnosis people would look me in the eye, trying to find some kind of fear,

and what they would see is their own fear reflected back at them. The bottom line is what you have to deal with is people's fear of being ill, fear of being generally compromised, fear of being outside of the circle of able-bodied people."

Money raised at this event helps fund local programs for those with Parkinson's, including innovative research, yoga classes, dance classes, support groups and intensive physical therapy. The Parkinson's Disease and Movement Disorder Center at Pennsylvania Hospital and Jefferson Hospital are beneficiaries of the significant sums raised at the annual golf outing.

"One of the mysteries is you never know when someone will contract the disease," continues Albert, whose own mother lived thirteen years after being diagnosed. "Parkinson's patients can live for many years. So it's our goal to provide support not only for those diagnosed with Parkinson's, but also for their families." She points out that some of the tournament proceeds go to the social workers themselves, supplementing mostly modest salaries, so they can invest their full energy in helping the families and care-partners learn how to best help people with Parkinson's.

"We've often thought of charging more per player, and scaling back to a more manageably-sized event, but while that might be equal in terms of our bottom line, it would expose far fewer people to what we are doing. In our opinion, knowledge of and awareness of the disease is just as important as the dollars raised."

"Whenever I see David Halpern or his mom, Arlene, I thank them for the tenacity they showed at the beginning," concludes Albert, thinking back to the man who initially proposed the golf tournament. "They felt a golf event benefiting Parkinson's research would gain a foothold, and they were right. Our committee owes them a debt of gratitude for their foresight."

So do thousands of people living with Parkinson's in Philadelphia, Delaware and southern New Jersey. They have a better chance of fighting this disease, or perhaps one day even living to see a cure for it, due to the significant funds being raised annually at this fine golf outing.

For more information visit: www.theparkinsoncouncil.org

The Patriot Foundation

PATRIOT

FOUNDATION.

Taking Care of Those Left Behind.

patriotfoundation.com

Former Illinois Governor and presidential candidate Adlai Stevenson died in 1965, nearly forty years before the Patriot Foundation was set up. Nevertheless, he managed to sum up their mission in a single, elegant sentence. "Patriotism is not a short, frenzied outburst of emotion, but the tranquil and steady dedication of a lifetime."

When a bomb, bullet, or other weapon shatters the life and well-being of an American soldier, the reverberation of the injury goes far beyond that individual's physical and psychological devastation. Recovery is measured in months, if not years. As the grievously injured start on the long road back to recovery, it usually falls upon the spouse to not only become the primary caregiver, but also the family breadwinner and parent-in-chief.

It is for these reasons, among many others, that the Patriot Foundation was founded in 2003, and has subsequently awarded over three million dollars in scholarship funds. The organization supports families of servicemen and women killed, wounded, and injured in the global war on terrorism. They provide scholarship funding and other aid for the children of soldiers at Ft. Bragg, North Carolina and points beyond. They also provide funding for childcare for the families of fallen and disabled soldiers whose surviving spouses need to obtain job training.

Hard to believe, but this vitally important cause might not have been discovered if not for an odd response to a simple question at a casual dinner gathering. "My wife Debbie asked our new neighbor Tanda Jarest over for a meal," begins Patriot

Foundation founder Spike Smith. "I asked her where her husband was, and she shrugged and said, 'Who knows?' I was puzzled until I found out he was a Special Forces operative, and his whereabouts were classified."

Eventually Smith, a Pinehurst, North Carolina businessman who had served in the Navy during the Vietnam era, met his globetrotting neighbor, Lieutenant Colonel Neal Jarest. Using some of his new neighbor's military connections, Smith, a former professional golfer, decided to add a charitable component to a professional golf tournament he had started the year prior. "Our first year we gave money solely to the unit scholarship fund at Fort Bragg. But shortly thereafter we decided to expand our reach, and began helping military fam-ilies throughout Fort Bragg and in other regions."

Chuck Deleot (pronounced like Elliot) is the president and chairman of the board of the Patriot Foundation. "Since 9/11, there have been upwards of half a million military personnel who have been seriously wounded, including huge numbers of individuals suffering from PTSD," explains the former Navy captain, who as a civilian became the technical director for the commander-in-chief of the Pacific Fleet. "These injuries occur not just in war zones, but in training exercises at home. The Patriot Foundation helps their families when they need it most."

Monies provided can be used not just for school tuition, but room, board, tutoring, a computer - basically anything authorized from a 529-plan education fund. Though the grants are limited, usually a few thousand dollars per family, the impact isn't. "Studies show that even a small financial window of opportunity can engender optimism among the youth of our military families," continues Deleot. "Money we provide exponentially increases the chances of a child going to college. These are families that struggle financially in the best of times. When a catastrophe strikes a military family, we want to provide the children a ray of hope for their future, and not feel discouraged they have no options to pursue an education." Deleot points out that the 'seed money' provided by the Patriot Foundation might spur a child to look for other grants and scholarships. The foundation might provide additional assistance the following year, and the year after that. It is through these small steps that the basis of a great education begins.

Much like the military itself, the Patriot Foundation is a lean, mean machine, with up to ninety-seven percent of all money collected going out to help the families in need. "We aren't as big or well-known as some of the more brand-name military causes," admits Deleot. "But I would be surprised to learn of any others that ran as efficiently."

Referring to their annual golf event, Spike Smith states that, "things really took off a few years in when we added an honoree to our dinner program. These important military commanders lent an air of gravitas, a seriousness of purpose, to our fundraising efforts. We immediately had more credibility, were able to raise much more money, and get more attention. As important as anything else, we now have these highly acclaimed, much decorated generals and other senior military personnel aware of us, and in our corner."

Their initial honoree in 2005 was Major General Chuck Swannack, former head of the 82nd Airborne Division at Fort Bragg. He was followed in 2006 by General Buck Kernan, who served as the Commander-in-Chief of the U.S. Joint Forces Command. They were followed by illustrious honorees like Admiral Mike Mullen, who served as Chairman of the Joint Chiefs of Staff, and General Ray Odierno, the Chief of Staff of the U.S. Army, among other extremely high-ranking military officials.

Smith takes pride in the fact that as a player, he qualified for three Senior British Opens, but is even prouder of his role in the creation of the Patriot Foundation. However, he is quick to hand off credit. "My wife Debbie and I laid the first few bricks, but Chuck Deleot is the man who built the structure. It is through his diligence, connections and hard work that we have evolved to this point. More importantly, he has laid the underpinning for future success, so this organization will continue to flourish long after he and I cease to be involved."

U.S. Army Special Operations and the XVIII Airborne Corps are among the military outfits that have created their own 501(c)3 charities, to better allow the Patriot Foundation to provide grants. Their inherent flexibility allows them to make emergency grants as needed. A tragic example: when twenty-two Navy SEALS were killed in a helicopter crash in Afghanistan in 2011, the foundation provided their children $125,000 in grants, plus an additional $30,000 for the children of the four airmen piloting the craft.

"In all my decades in the military, I have never seen brighter, more motivated or more capable individuals than what we have today," states Deleot. "These men and women could be a success in any field of endeavor. They choose to serve our nation, protect our freedom and keep us safe."

Concludes Deleot, "It isn't just our obligation. It is actually our honor to support our deserving military families. Our belief is that a strong military insures our freedoms, and a weaker military invites chaos."

The 'weakest' members of a military family, the children, often left in the lurch when a catastrophic injury befalls a parent, will always be the focus of the exquisite work being done by the Patriot Foundation.

For more information visit: www.patriotfoundation.com

The Randy Jones Invitational

Former Major League pitcher Randy Jones hung up his cleats nearly thirty-five years ago, after a decade-long career in the big leagues. His heyday was the bicentennial year of 1976, when he won twenty-two games and the Cy Young Award as the ace of the San Diego Padres.

Owing to the passage of time, despite two All-Star appearances and a hundred career wins, only the most dedicated baseball fan could identify Jones walking down the street. That is, everywhere but San Diego, where "Junkman" Jones is revered as a cultural and sports icon. He's recognized and approached on a daily basis, his uniform number has been retired, and he does television and radio work for the team while simultaneously lending his name to five separate barbecue joints dotted around the Padres home stadium, Petco Park.

Given his singular status around town, (the other local touchstones of athletic excellence, Junior Seau of the Chargers and Tony Gwynn of the Padres are no longer living) it comes as no surprise that one of the most popular, not to mention innovative

and effective charity golf tournament formats found in southern California, is known as the Randy Jones Invitational.

"For more than thirty years I've been playing in charity golf events, many hundreds over time, helping them raise money on that day," begins Jones, born in Fullerton, little more than an hour north of San Diego. "But with the unique format of the Randy Jones Invitational, we can help hundreds of events at once. I loved the idea, and signed on right away."

San Diegans Curtis and Linda Gandy came up with the concept. Linda spent more than twenty years in the San Diego Chargers organization, and volunteered at numerous charity golf events. Curtis spent thirty years as the sales manager for a contracting company, and as an avid golfer played in charity events regularly. Shortly after his birth, their son Brandon spent the better part of two years in and out of the local children's hospital with various medical issues. It was during those dark times that the couple started to see the enormous

power of fundraising using golf as the engine.

They met Randy in autumn of 2012 and proposed a novel idea. Instead of a charity golf tournament culminating with a tepid round of applause for the winning foursome as they collected their crystal or trophies, they suggested that these local events become a springboard to a de facto charity championship. In other words, the winners (subsequently amended to include the second and third place team also) advance and play in another event at no cost. This event was dubbed the Randy Jones Invitational, and the only way into this elite field was with a high finish at a qualifying charity event in San Diego County.

Initiated after the 2013 charity tournament season, four hundred foursomes descended on San Diego's popular Sycuan Resort for the inaugural Randy Jones Invitational. Though each team played only one day in their flight, the event took ten days to contest. The top thirty-six teams of those initial four hundred then qualified to play in the finals at nearby Torrey Pines. The winning team was richly rewarded. The charity they originally played for received a check for ten thousand dollars, their four names were inscribed on a perpetual trophy housed in the San Diego Hall of Champions, and best of all was a trip to Carmel via private aircraft for a weekend at the Pebble Beach Resort.

The scramble format has always been the charity event standard because it is far less stressful than playing one's own ball for eighteen straight holes. Jones

$10,000 Putting Challenge

SOUTHWEST GREENS
GOLF SOLUTIONS

RANDY JONES

February 22, 2015

Pay to the order of Grand Prize Winner $ 10,000.00
Ten Thousand Dollars and.............. 00/100

Congratulations!

was intrigued by the fact that before his eponymous event was created there wasn't a method to crown an overall local scramble champion, and he sought to bring legitimacy to this sometimes loose form of golf. At his events, there are no mulligans or strings for sale to enhance a team's score, and there's an official and a scorer located on each hole to keep things above board. Jones and the Gandys had transformed the "hit and giggle" format of scramble golf into something serious, quantifiable and competitive. Far more importantly, they gave golfers all around the region an extra incentive to sign up for the charity golf event of their choice.

"People ask me if they can get in our event all the time," recounts Jones, who finished his pitching career with the New York Mets in 1982. "I just tell them to go play in a charity event and qualify, that's the only way in. I've even met guys who finished just out of the top three spots in the event they entered, and then entered another charity tournament in the hopes they could get that top three finish and get into ours. These examples show how effective our event is in getting golfers in the area to support all manner of charity tournaments."

Curt and Linda Gandy get the same desperation requests. "People call and ask if they can pay to get in the invitational, and we simply tell them that there's no charge to participate. But— you have to play in a charity event elsewhere, and hopefully have a high finish," explains Linda.

The question: how can Jones and the organizers afford to foot the bill for nearly sixteen hundred golfers at no cost to the players themselves? The answer is a single word, which happens to be the most important word in all of charity golf-sponsorship.

"We are indebted to the Sycuan Golf Resort and Casino, which hosts our group for ten straight days. We have amazing corporate partners like EDCO, West-Pac Wealth Partners, Wells Fargo, the Padres, BH Gold, Corky's Pest Control, Cox Business, SD Trophies, and Attention Getters, among others, who see the value of getting their names out to this affluent crowd, and also love the fact we're helping to raise so much money for so many worthy causes," relates Curt Gandy.

There's no empirical way of measuring the positive effect of the Randy Jones Invitational on the coffers of all these charities, but consider this-if the incentive of earning one's way into this event is enough to get even a single foursome to sign up at a charity event that they would otherwise eschew that's perhaps six hundred dollars to that charity. Now multiply that number by hundreds of charity events around the region, and it's easy to surmise that the additional dollars raised annually goes into the middle six figures.

Any way you look at it, the Randy Jones Invitational is a magnificent innovation, because it benefits so many other magnificent causes concurrently.

For more information visit: www.randyjonesinvitational.com

Stater Bros. Charities
Dave Stockton Heroes Challenge

A perspective on exclusivity: there have been approximately fifteen thousand major league baseball players throughout history, nearly six thousand men have worn NBA uniforms, and about four thousand individuals have reached the summit of Mt. Everest. But since the first one was awarded in 1863, there have been fewer than thirty-five hundred recipients of the Congressional Medal of Honor, the single most prestigious military combat award that America bestows.

Simply put, it is the highest U.S. military honor, awarded by Congress to a member of the armed forces for gallantry and bravery in combat at the risk of life above and beyond the call of duty. The Medal of Honor is the ultimate tribute for a soldier who has seen combat, only given to those brave and selfless souls who have risked their own lives to save others. "There is no higher award that America can bestow upon a member of our military. It's not surprising to learn that about two-thirds of them are presented posthumously." So begins Jack H. Brown, the chairman and CEO of Stater Bros. Markets, and the de facto host of one of the most soul-stirring charity golf events in the nation.

There are many hundreds of high-end charity

golf events, contested on stunning venues, with gourmet cuisine, top-shelf liquor, gift bags suited for the Oscars, celebrities in every foursome or at every table. But the Heroes Challenge offers something few events can: honest-to-goodness Medal of Honor recipients, and there is no group living that deserves the respect, admiration and downright awe that these Medal of Honor recipients receive.

It's not surprising that Stater Bros. Markets is the driving force behind this superb event. The CEO is a Navy vet himself, born on Flag Day. But the legacy extends way beyond his more than thirty-five year tenure at Stater Bros.

This eighty-year-old company was founded by twins Leo and Cleo Stater, World War II veterans who came back from battle and expanded what had been two small grocery markets into the expansive chain it became. That initial pair of modest stores, located in the towns of Redlands and Yucaipa, has since exploded to almost 170 supermarkets throughout southern California. It is the single largest private employer in the Inland Empire, some sixty miles east of Los Angeles, with eighteen thousand employees, and it is also the largest privately-owned supermarket chain in Southern California.

Susan Atkinson is the president of Stater Bros. Charities, the company's philanthropic arm. "We were able to do smaller projects through our many store locations but wanted to help out in a bigger way, so we formed Stater Bros. Charities in 2008. It was important we form this charitable entity, because we were receiving upwards of four thousand individual charity requests annually," states Atkinson, who has also served as the vice-president of corporate affairs for many years. "We donate in excess of fifteen million dollars

annually to schools, hospitals, food banks, and other vital causes, in addition to our support of the Medal of Honor Foundation."

The genesis of what became the Heroes Challenge was Stater Bros. Markets serving as a major sponsor at the 1999 Medal of Honor Convention held in Riverside, California. "I asked Dave Stockton to be my guest at the dinner," recalls Jack Brown. "Not only have we been friends since our childhood in nearby San Bernardino, our dads were good friends also. We both found it incredibly thrilling and humbling to be around heroes of this magnitude. Dave was blown away by the event, which included eighty Medal of Honor recipients, and two at our very table. We sat with Korean War veteran Joseph Rodriguez, and Vietnam War veteran Ronald Ray, both Medal of Honor recipients and both avid golfers!"

Stockton, a two-time winner of the PGA Championship and the winning 1991 Ryder Cup captain, decided then and there to create an event that would raise money

for the Medal of Honor Society's scholarship program which raises funds for the children of the award's recipients.

Stockton Golf, the multi-faceted company that Dave operates with his sons, Ron and Dave Jr., has been participating at events at Medal of Honor conventions and fundraisers since 2000. These events include clinics, a tournament, and at times, a selection of Tour professionals from the Champions Tour and the LPGA. For his devotion to the cause, Stockton was honored as their Distinguished Citizen of the Year at the 2006 convention in Boston. In fact, Stockton's passion for the cause led him to encourage the PGA Tour to award lifetime passes to any tour event for all living Medal of Honor recipients.

The eighty Medal of Honor recipients in attendance at the 1999 convention in Riverside have dwindled to less than seventy during the ensuing years. While the World War II, Korean War, and even Vietnam-era vets are dwindling, the overall numbers are bolstered somewhat by a newer generation of recipients, veterans of the Gulf War, and the conflicts in Iraq and Afghanistan.

Victoria Club in Riverside, California and Redlands Country Club in Redlands, California have played host to the annual Heroes Challenge event. Because of the magnitude and influence of the Stater Bros. Markets chain, their loyal vendors are among the tournament's most ardent supporters. "It goes way beyond the golf, the golf clinic, the prizes and the setting. It's all about the Medal of Honor recipients," states Stockton, who won his major championships in 1970

and 1976. "Most people will never meet a Medal of Honor recipient in their lives. At this event we always have a half dozen."

This unique event also honors up to five 'community heroes,' who are then able to designate a donation from Stater Bros. Charities to a charity of their choice.

Pepsi Beverages Company, Frito-Lay, Anheuser-Busch Inc., Coca-Cola, Dr. Pepper Snapple Group, General Mills, MillerCoors, The Performance Group and Young's Market Company are among the companies in attendance and sending foursomes to the event. This is a high-powered day that attracts senior executives at the CEO and CFO level, virtually all of whom claim it to be the best charity golf event of the year. While entry fees are a private matter, suffice it to say rubbing elbows or maybe even playing golf with these true American heroes doesn't come cheap.

After all, it's not often when star golfers and major winners like Lee Trevino, Hubert Green, Morgan Pressel, Larry Nelson and Paul Azinger play second fiddle at a country club. But when the Medal of Honor recipients are in the house, the pros are bowled over just like everybody else.

The Heroes Challenge is twenty-seven holes over two days. With only a few hundred people in attendance at this private event, there are no crowds at the clinics, everyone gets personal attention, and every attendee can meet every luminary, be they golf stars or combat heroes. "It's a very impactful event for those lucky enough to participate," offers Susan Atkinson. Multiple millions have been raised since the event's inception, and though the original Stater brothers, Cleo and Leo, are no longer around, they would doubtless approve of their company's involvement. Concludes Jack Brown, "I'm sure they would be very proud and impressed."

Just like everyone else fortunate enough to take part.

For more information visit: www.heroeschallenge.org

Sunshine Through Golf
Foundation Outing

Chicago's Sunshine Through Golf Foundation Outing is distinctive for all the things it doesn't have.

There's no fleet of golf carts on hand, nor a surfeit of players milling in the parking lot or tournament staging area. There's not a raffle ticket or mulligan to purchase, nor a complicated rule sheet to help parse the details of the scramble, shamble, or bramble format.

What it does have is a modestly-sized and serious group of committed players, who (mostly) walk, (mostly) with caddies in tow, and play their own golf ball on some of the most venerable clubs in greater Chicago. Illustrious grounds like Rich Harvest Farms, Beverly, Knollwood, Shoreacres and Exmoor have played host to the group since its 2002 inception.

Sheldon Solow, along with close friend Tom Allison, is the co-founder of this uniquely intimate event. "I've been running charity golf tournaments for more than twenty-five years," explains the native Chicagoan, who's only lived outside his home turf for the three years he was attending Harvard Law School. "I've come to the conclusion there are a few main reasons as to why people play in these events. They want to support the cause, they like the course, like the host, feel it's a good value for their charitable dollars, or feel it's good for their business relationships. Our wonderful tournament committee serves a vital role, as they spread the word about us in their own circles, and help insure a full field. One major difference is that while many charity events are populated with twice-a-season golfers, we tend to attract discriminating, serious players."

Nowadays stellar organizations like Folds of

Honor and Wounded Warriors are well known. But the century-old Chicago District Golf Association, ostensibly the "parent company" of the Sunshine Through Golf Foundation, has been supporting our returning troops since 1944. "The CDGA began funneling monies towards returning vets during World War One," continues Solow, a partner in a major law firm, "but it became an official cause for the organization during World War Two."

Over time, the CDGA's charitable arm expanded to include disabled and economically disadvantaged kids in addition to the veterans. The Sunshine through Golf Foundation funds upwards of two hundred clinics annually throughout greater Chicago, no trifling number considering the brevity of the Midwestern golf season.

Additionally, they built and continue to maintain a three-hole golf course at the CDGA's headquarters, which serves a dual purpose. Not only are the kids and vets welcome to play what's known as the Sunshine Golf Course, with wheelchairs, walkers and leg braces as common a site as flagsticks and tee markers, but the course also serves as a turfgrass research facility, with a full-time agronomist on the CDGA staff. "Our agronomist is available to help area superintendents combat any exotic or little-known syndromes that might be negatively impacting that member club or facility," explains Solow. "So serious research is being conducted in the field of turfgrass and their diseases, and consequently hundreds of courses and clubs in the region can benefit from this expertise, and enjoy better playing conditions."

While luxurious fairway grass is always nice, in the big picture bringing opportunities to those less fortunate is at the beating heart of the Sunshine Through Golf Foundation. "Many of these kids have self-esteem issues, and have dealt with setbacks in life. They feel like they're less worthy than their more able-bodied peers, and have myriad problems, above and beyond their physical and economic reality," states the senior director of the foundation, Brittany Ottolini. "When they absorb the instruction and eventually hit a real golf shot, make solid contact and get the ball in the air, their joy is palpable," continues Solow. "So is the pride and relief you sometimes see in the faces of their parents. I tell our volunteers, board members and donors the same thing; we're not curing cancer and we're not eradicating the many problems in the world. But come to a clinic just one time. When you see how kids react and respond to positive feedback and performance improvement, how excited they get when they achieve even a modicum of success, you'll support this cause for life."

Thanks to the support of the CDGA, which benefits from eighty thousand dues-paying members, the Sunshine Through Golf Foundation is able to put about ninety cents of every dollar raised towards their programs; just a dime goes to overhead.

"The irony is that the CDGA organizes dozens of amateur golf tournaments annually, but they were unsure of how to run a charity event, and if it would be worth our collective efforts," states Allison, a financial consultant. "We came up with this less is more concept, and thankfully it has been a major success. The foundation has other fund-raising components, but this is really the bell cow of our organization. We are thankful it's been as well-received as it has."

Well aware that charity golf events can wither and die, the principals, aged sixty-ish, have an eye towards the future. They are recruiting fresh blood for their committee, and because the field has been made up primarily of their peers, they are intent on making sure the next generation of tournament participants becomes enamored of the simple elegance of their annual event.

Solow, who for a decade prior to his Sunshine involvement ran a large-scale charity golf event for a brand-name cause with all the bells and whistles, an event that has subsequently gone by the wayside, concludes with a carnivorous comparison.

"A delicious hamburger can be one of the most enjoyable things you can eat. But a well-prepared sirloin or filet is equally good, and many would suggest even more satisfying. They are both appealing, both delicious. However, an argument can be made that the filet is a more enriching, more sophisticated experience. That's how we describe our outing."

Seems as though their regular participants come back eagerly, annually, always hungry for more.

For more information
visit: www.sunshinethroughgolf.org

Swing for Sight Golf Tournament and The Ultra Speed Golf Challenge for Ocular Melanoma

SWING
for
SIGHT
Ocular Melanoma

Ocular melanoma. Odds are you've never heard of it before, but also that you can figure out pretty quickly what it's all about.

This type of eye cancer is exceedingly rare, as only about two thousand cases are reported annually. Compared to nearly half a million combined cases of breast cancer and prostate cancer diagnosed each year, ocular melanoma is highly unusual. Much like Tim Scott, an amazing athlete and speed golfer, who was diagnosed with the disease in 2012.

Current research shows a correlation between the unprotected eye and the possibility of developing ocular melanoma. So in addition to being steadfast in the use of sunglasses that protect against ultra-violet radiation, individuals should be willing to get their eyes dilated when visiting their ophthalmologist or eye care professional. "The more they can examine the eye, the better chance for early detection," offers Scott.

Scott considers himself fortunate, and not only

because his ability and fitness level allow him to shoot near par while running eighteen holes in the time most cart-tethered golfers are barely halfway through the front nine. "Sometimes there are no symptoms at all, but I felt a curtain, for lack of a better term, slowly coming across my right eye. The doctor discovered a tumor, which had grown enough to affect my vision."

If undiscovered, the eye cancer will almost invariably spread to the liver, a curious pathway which science cannot explain. In most cases it becomes fatal. Enucleation, or removal of the eye, is the most drastic option. In lieu of removal, a patient can opt for either plaque brachytherapy or proton beam therapy. Scott opted for the former, which involves sewing a dime-sized patch strewn with radioactive "seeds" onto the eyeball for five days. The latter in-

volves wearing a protective mask similar to what a hockey goalie wears, and having the cancer-killing beam shot directly into the afflicted eye.

Tim Scott has retained peripheral vision in his right eye, though his straight-on vision and depth perception have been compromised. "Simple things like walking down stairs, pouring a cup of coffee or using a remote control aren't as easy as they once were," admits the longtime schoolteacher. "But I'm getting better with practice."

One can only imagine the amount of practice it took for Scott to become so proficient at speed golf. Even with the eye patch he now wears to mitigate double vision, he can still burn up a golf course in less than fifty minutes. He's still shooting scores that ninety-five percent of dedicated golfers could only dream of, and he does so under his own power, in a quarter of the time. His best score is seventy shots in forty-two minutes, which added together result in a speed golf score of 112.

Improbably, the three founders of Speed Golf International grew up in Eugene, Oregon, and all of them graduated high school in 1981. Scott and his friends Chris Smith and Jim Kosciolek were members of their respective high school golf teams, Scott and Smith going on to play in college and eventually becoming PGA professionals. It was a natural fit, as Scott and Smith were scratch players and avid, dedicated trail runners. Smith eventually became a Guinness world record holder. In 2005 he completed eighteen holes in forty-four minutes, carrying just six clubs. His score was an astonishing sixty-five strokes, resulting in a speed golf score of 109.

"Speed golf makes you a better golfer," explains the fifty-something Scott, who began competing in speed golf events in 1998. "Golfers generally take too much time, and waste too much time. Speed golf makes it a reactive game, not an analytical game. You learn to work the ball different ways, hit shots harder or easier, owing to the fact you are carrying just a handful of clubs to maintain pace. Look at it this way: A PGA tour player can only make a twenty foot putt once in ten tries. Amateurs will only make one of twenty. Therefore, one needn't read the putt from all sides beforehand, as it's unlikely to go in regardless! Jog or run briskly between shots, but not so fast that you're panting for breath when you arrive at the ball. Eschew practice swings. Go with your first instinct. Let your subconscious take over as you feel the distance you need to hit the ball. Once you're on the green, size up your putt at a glance, hit it, finish quickly and get to the next hole. That's speed golf at its essence."

Scott put the essence of this niche sport on display at magnificent Bandon Dunes resort in his native Oregon in 2013, raising funds and awareness for ocular melanoma. He played all eighty-five holes at the resort in less than four and a half hours, raising nearly twenty thousand dollars. That led him to join forces with Melody Burchett in 2015, joining her Swing for Sight golf event in Napa, California.

"Most gatherings of ocular melanoma patients are something of a downer," begins Burchett, who was diagnosed in 2010, and like Tim Scott, chose to undergo plaque brachytherapy. "Doctors give presentations regarding whatever little progress they've made in terms of research, and friends you might have met at previous events might not be there. The mortality rate of those who've

contracted the disease is around fifty percent. So I decided to stage an upbeat golf event, and to attract both patients and potential supporters, I chose a 'bucket list' destination in Napa."

Tim Scott recruited four individuals and one additional team of three players, who opted for a relay-style speed golf marathon at Burchett's Swing for Sight event. While there were dozens of players registered for the main charity golf event at a nearby course, the eight speed golfers committed to not only playing for twelve hours dawn-to-dusk, but each of them also pledged to bring in at least five thousand dollars in donations. Nobody covered more ground than famed ultra-marathoner Karl Meltzer, who has won dozens of hundred-mile races. Meltzer melted the golf course, playing a mind-boggling 229 holes (almost thirteen full rounds) averaging under an hour per circuit. Tim Scott was a relative slacker at his own event, managing 144 holes (eight full rounds) before tight hamstrings reduced him to painful jogging, then shuffling along, giving up the ghost after about eleven hours.

The speed demons were in justifiable pain, but it was Melody Burchett who was crying at the post-tournament dinner, overcome with the magnanimity and awe-inspiring endurance of Tim Scott and his crew.

"When I think about the dedication and the amount of energy that these marvelous athletes expended to raise money and awareness of this little-known disease, it gets me choked up, and feeling very emotional," concludes Burchett. "I doubt one person in a million would be willing or able to golf themselves into exhaustion over twelve hours, covering fifty miles or more and taking a thousand swings. Tim and his colleagues are a rare breed, as rare as the disease itself."

Due to the dearth of cases, funding for and awareness of ocular melanoma are minimal. But if the dedication of the small cadre of doctors and research scientists studying it can someday approach the intense focus and commitment to the cause as shown by the elite cadre of speed golfers that Tim Scott calls friends and colleagues, perhaps one day a cure will be forthcoming.

For more information visit: www.acureinsight.org

The Tiger Golf Gathering

What do current and former PGA Tour players Lucas Glover, Jonathan Byrd and Charles Warren have in common? Familiarity with the winner's circle, that's for sure. The trio has combined for more than a dozen victories on the PGA and Web.com tours. Love of alma mater is another common thread. All three played and thrived at Clemson University, located in the lively town of the same name in the northwest part of South Carolina, midway between Atlanta and Charlotte.

Thirdly and most importantly, they were the principals who quite by happenstance turned the original notion of a campus reunion with their beloved golf coach and a humble charity idea into a finely tuned engine of efficient fundraising. The beneficiary is the Clemson golf team, which is a non-revenue sport for the university.

"We had been out on tour for a while, playing in other charity events hosted by our peers," begins Charles Warren, who spent fifteen years as a touring professional before entering the insurance business. "We wanted to do something to honor Clemson and our coach Larry Penley, who was like a second father to all of us. Our original goal was simple; to raise funds for a short game facility, the kind we wished we had access to as students. We also knew it would be a recruiting tool for Larry. Then we won the national championship shortly thereafter, and the Tiger Golf Gathering was off and running."

For a charity event to find almost instantaneous success generally requires a bit of luck and timing. Consider that Clemson captured its first-ever NCAA golf championship in 2003, just one year after the inaugural Tiger Golf Gathering. That excitement reverberated for years, and when things calmed down a bit, founding father Lucas Glover captured the U.S. Open in 2009, creating another tsunami of enthusiasm.

Todd Lankford is the volunteer president of the Tiger Golf Gathering Foundation, which raises funds for both the men's and women's golf programs at Clemson, helps fund the school's PGM (Professional Golf Management) Program, and also provides funds for the South Carolina Junior Golf Association.

"First off, a school like Clemson has such a loyal alumni base, myself included," begins the Charlotte, North Carolina business executive. "It's one of the major universities in the Carolinas, and so many graduates look back fondly on the time they spent there, they try and stay close to the school. Add in the fact that so many southern businessmen love golf, and we have this perfect formula for support."

It's no secret that football and basketball are the main revenue-producing sports at any college or university, helping to fund the bulk of the other athletic programs. "We were first out of the gate at Clemson, raising additional funds for golf, and now several other of the non-revenue sports programs are attempting the same thing," states Lankford.

What's left unsaid is the built-in advantage of golf as a participatory endeavor. Not many aquatics supporters care to dive in the pool with Clemson's swim team. It's the rare lacrosse lover willing to sprint down the field cradling their stick. But the golfers love to golf, be back on campus, and rub elbows with the current team members, the three founders, and another trio of Clemson golfers, Ben Martin, D.J. Trahan and Kyle Stanley, who have all won on the PGA Tour.

Another factor in the success of this event is the fact that the Clemson golfers on tour are wonderful ambassadors for their cause. "These guys are in pro-ams all the time, have warm, friendly personalities, and often endear themselves to their amateur partners," explains Lankford. "We occasionally get checks out of the blue from people in different parts of the country, no Clemson affiliation whatsoever. They met one of our guys, enjoyed their experience and decided to support their favorite charity."

The women's golf team has only been in existence a few years, but having these delightful young women as part of the Tiger Golf Gathering is an added bonus, as are the singular auction items the night of the big dinner. Lots of marquee charity events offer cool experiences at auction: rounds at exclusive courses, Super Bowl tickets, etc. But combine the lure of the tour with the motivation of Clemson's high-profile alumni golfers, and the sum total can only be described as one-of-a-kind. "We auction the chance to caddy for Lucas, Jonathan, Charles or one of their tour buddies during the Tuesday practice round of the Wells Fargo Championship in Charlotte," states Lankford, referring to one of the PGA Tour's most prestigious titles. "We auction a golf round with Ben and Charles, followed by a wine dinner with them both in downtown Greenville. These are incredible experiences, and bidding is always robust, to say the least!"

Besides the noble cause, the event finds support because it's just plain fun. A Thursday round among the amateurs, the blowout party and big auction that evening, a round featuring all the pedigreed tour players (and the awe-inspiring abilities of the current Clemson team) on Friday.

"We're very fortunate that these were young men just starting their careers when they founded this charity, and they continue to find success in professional golf and the business world. Moreover they remain just as passionate about the cause more than a dozen years later. Thanks to their efforts and our entire team of volunteers we've raised in excess of one and a half million dollars." Lankford continues by stating that the ripple effect helps the university as a whole. "Because our golf program is high-profile, and garners this support, it spills over into other areas. People end up donating to Clemson itself, not just the Tiger Golf Gathering, and it has a positive effect across the board."

"If someone had told me fifteen years ago that our little fundraiser was going to grow to this size and scope, I wouldn't have imagined it possible," concludes Charles Warren. "It just goes to show when you get people together with a common goal, a common bond and real passion. Anything becomes possible."

Ideas evolve in ways you cannot foretell. Three young professional golfers decide to go back to the alma mater, hang out with their old coach, see their teammates, and contribute a few bucks. More than a dozen years later, the fundraiser they began on a whim continues to grow.

For more information visit: www.tigergolfgathering.com

Treetops Charity Fall Invitational

Michigan's Most Spectacular Resort
GOLF • SKI • SPA

One of the biggest challenges facing the Michigan golf industry is the idea that they offer too much value. This counterintuitive theory is espoused not by some crackpot outsider, but by native Michigander Kevin McKinley; a PGA professional, the longtime director of golf at Treetops Resort, and a man who knows of what he speaks.

"People from out of state are astonished to realize that for about five hundred dollars total, we offer great tee gifts, three days of championship golf, two nights lodging, multiple breakfasts, lunches and dinners that feature open bars. They think it's all too good to be true. Until they arrive, first-timers who might be from Florida, Texas, or Nevada can't comprehend the beauty, scenery, challenge and quality of our autumn product. They figure the courses must be mediocre at best."

Anything but. Treetops, with its eighty-one scintillating holes, is a sterling example of why, in recent decades, Michigan has vaulted to the forefront as a summertime golf destination. The Treetops Charity Fall Invitational, sponsored by Pepsi, has been in existence for nearly thirty years. It takes place with brilliant autumn weather, well past the peak of the summer season. Because resort traffic dwindles come October, Treetops can discount the event heavily. This helps attract some four hundred players, and make a significant donation to the needy beneficiaries.

The event's net proceeds benefit as many as fifteen or more charities in Otsego County, a rural area to the north where income lags behind even the rest of the hard-hit Michigan economy. The main beneficiaries include the local hospital and hospice, and the local foster care program. They also support the community foundation, which provides grants to community-minded projects and awards scholarships to worthy students. Relates McKinley, "We try and make life a little easier for those living in and around Gaylord, which is the main town in the county."

McKinley's decade of tenure at the resort has featured what he refers to as a laser-like focus in regards to giving. "When we allocate funds to the Habitat for Humanity, for example, we know exactly how many new windows, doors or fixtures our donation is paying for. When we give money to the Reach Out and Read Program, which benefits children, we know that we are helping them purchase exactly five or eight hundred new books, depending on the year."

While Otsego County residents only comprise about five percent of the field in any given year, most players hail from other parts of Michigan, with representatives from as many as fifteen other states and countries sprinkled among the participants. "Some people come because they're charitably oriented," continues the pro. "Others come because they love the resort, the parties, or even the daily skins pool, where they can win a few bucks. When you put four hundred people together, there is no single reason as to their motivation."

That motivation rarely wanes. The event is rife with repeat customers, and a significant percentage count their participation in decades, not just years. "We announce our twenty-year participants at one of the dinners," explains McKinley, "and the roll call is always fifty names minimum, usually more."

The growth of the Treetops Charity Fall Invitational, which began in 1987, is commensurate with the growth of the resort itself. It began as a two-day event on one golf course, and has subsequently grown to a three-day event on a trio of excellent tracks. It is likely the only tournament in the country featuring a rotation of courses designed by Robert Trent Jones, Sr., Tom Fazio, and Rick Smith.

"We play as two foursomes per hole, which fosters amazing camaraderie," continues McKinley, who has spent his entire career in his home state. "Instead of being insulated within your own group of buddies, you are meeting at least a dozen other participants during the course of three days of play. Multiply that by a decade or more of participation, and it's easy to see why this has become an informal networking event, as a significant percentage of our participants have met, played with and befriended numerous others. It's become almost like a reunion every fall."

Another great attribute is the use of five sets of tees, so teams comprised of players of different ages, genders and abilities can still compete on a level playing field. "There's no need to stack a team with scratch golfers," states McKinley. "Players within the team play from the appropriate teeing ground, so everyone can contribute." Not only can they contribute, but because each team must use four drives per player during each tournament round, each of the teammates must contribute to the competitive cause.

"Our challenge," concludes the director of golf, "is convincing those unfamiliar with Treetops to come up here in the first place. Once they arrive on property, it's gratifying to see their reaction. The response is never 'Why did I come?' but more along the lines of 'Why didn't I come until now?'"

For more information visit: www.treetops.com

The Troops Direct Golf Challenge

It began with a simple care package and morphed into a lifetime cause.

Aaron Negherbon (pronounced "near-bon") had sent off a package of toiletries and other comfort items to a close friend, a Marine Corps captain stationed in Afghanistan. "He wrote to thank me, and admitted he felt compelled to share everything with the troops under his command, that they needed it more than he did. That really got me thinking."

Not to mention got him moving. Despite having no military background of his own, he threw his energies into founding TroopsDirect. Since 2010, more than a half-million pounds of directly requested operational and medical supplies have been shipped across the United States and to four other continents. "There are other organizations that provide comfort items to our service people," explains the Oakland, California native, thinking back to that initial care package that precipitated his career change from the mortgage industry to founding TroopsDirect. "However, we are the only ones providing mission-critical items like stretchers, tourniquets, helmets, body armor, antennas, walkie-talkies, radio parts, GPS components, and other crucial equipment that allow our soldiers to do their job in the most efficient manner. Our goal is to enhance mission effectiveness and increase survivability rates."

Why doesn't the government properly supply our troops? It's often the first question asked by those solicited for either monetary or material donations.

"There are several main reasons," continues the forty-something Negherbon, who was in the automotive business as well as mortgages before founding TroopsDirect. "It has to do with budget cuts, bureaucracy, choke points in the

supply system, and the fact that when the government can respond, there's rarely a supply depot in proximity to where the need is greatest. What might take six or eight weeks for the government to supply we can usually get to the front line in seven to ten days. One of the driving forces we have is to make sure our soldiers aren't constantly repairing equipment that's essentially beyond repair, or jerry-rigging something with duct tape and safety pins to keep it operational. With all they do for us, we owe them new, unbroken and undamaged equipment so they can do their jobs right."

Another example might be with special forces units, needing to quickly deploy to a global hot spot. Sometimes the government cannot equip them quickly enough, so TroopsDirect steps in and gets them what they need, stat.

What began as a single warehouse operation in his hometown of Oakland has evolved into a drop-ship organization where trusted suppliers fulfill orders and use numerous locations as shipping points. Negherbon has developed delivery systems through UPS, DHL, Federal Express, the postal service and long-haul trucking operations, depending on whether the equipment is due stateside or bound for overseas. All of this comes at a great cost, and thanks to the concerted efforts of all involved, the organization has raised well in excess of five million dollars worth of equipment and monetary donations since inception, and they have doubled their donations every year of their existence. "This is what I live and breathe, twenty-five hours a day, eight days a week," states the USC graduate, who serves as the executive director, paying himself a modest salary on an irregular basis.

Though he personally prefers baseball to golf, the founder realized a golf tournament would be a key component in growing the organization. All charities hope to raise awareness in addition to needed funds, but because TroopsDirect is still in a nascent stage, Negherbon goes to imaginative lengths to ensure that his players develop a greater understanding of the military life.

Anyone who has ever played in a shotgun-start golf event is familiar with the pro or tournament organizer droning into the microphone before play begins, going over rules, long drive holes, closest-to-the-pin contests, etc. Not so here.

Bona fide drill sergeants are imported to ready the "troops" for their on-course battle, and woe to the sloppy player with an untucked shirt, untied shoe, cockeyed cap, or any other infraction that catches the eye and invokes the ire of these professional intimidators. Slovenly golfers are systematically and harshly dressed down by these enlisted men. "The only thing they don't do is order pushups," concedes Negherbon. "Some of our players are older, maybe out of shape, so we don't push it too far."

Golfers don't have to venture too far on the course to find authentic military weaponry, including a sniper rifle with scope, to gauge the distance on certain tee shots. They encounter bunkers outlined in the same orange neon chalk that our soldiers use to warn their comrades about the possibility of roadside bombs. At one hole there's even a fully equipped bulletproof vest, laden with body armor, ammo and other standard issue equipment to try on. Fortunately, no one is expected to make a golf swing while wearing this fifty-pound accoutrement.

Despite it being a relatively new tournament, the patrons absolutely embraced the concept, and more than $100,000 was raised in its first iteration, with projections for triple that amount in the encore event.

"These men and women volunteer to serve our country. I feel it's my duty to help give them what they need so they can survive, fulfill their mission, and get back home

to their families and loved ones. On the one hand, I wish an organization like TroopsDirect didn't need to exist," concludes the founder, thoughtfully. "But that said, I love what I do, and can't wait to get to the office every day."

By the same token, hundreds of thousands of troops, stationed stateside and in the harshest corners of the globe, are grateful that Aaron can't wait to get to the office. He makes their oft-unbearable burden just a little easier to deal with.

For more information
visit: www.troopsdirect.org

The Vitale
Memorial Charity Golf Tournament

Most of us go off to work every morning and never give a thought in regards to our safe return home. But for a police officer, there is no such thing as a routine shift. The Vitale Family, originally from Revere, Massachusetts, a blue-collar community just a few miles north of Boston, know that sad fact all too well.

Their much beloved brother Harold lost his life while on duty more than thirty years ago. His end of watch occurred during what should have been a routine traffic stop in the wee hours of June 18th, 1985. He was murdered by a callous teenager; an aggressive, indifferent driver with multiple moving violations, who was outraged by his perceived persecution by the local police department. The driver rolled up his window suddenly, trapping officer Vitale's arm in the car. He sped away, dragging him along, and shortly thereafter slammed him into a signpost. Harold was forty-two, happily married and the father of three. He was a veteran, a gifted auto mechanic, and an exceptional brother and son. Very few days have passed over more than three decades when his family does not think of him, what he meant to them, and what he meant to the community at large.

Although he wasn't trained as a first responder, according to his family he was always the first responder: the first to lend a hand, assist with a task, change a tire, or help with a home repair project. He was a fixture at the traditional Sunday dinner at their parent's home, as well as the never-ending cavalcade of birthdays, christenings, anniversaries and the like that are hallmarks of large families everywhere.

Harold was towards the middle of the birth order of the eight Vitale siblings, and served as the family linchpin. "We all felt accountable to Harold. If we were going to miss or skip a family event it better be for a good reason, or he would let us hear about it," relates youngest brother Les Vitale.

It seems as though police are in the news these days

for all the wrong reasons. Police brutality and wrongful deaths garner many headlines. But Harold made a point of showing a friendly face, especially to young people. He would give them rides in his cruiser or even on the back of his motorcycle, and attempted to illustrate that a policeman is your friend. It wasn't hard work for him; Harold was everybody's friend.

The golf tournament was the brainchild of Harold's widow Eileen and his older brother Dick. "Several years after the incident, Eileen volunteered at a golf tournament benefitting the organization C.O.P.S., which is an acronym for Concerns of Police Survivors," explains Les Vitale, an accountant by profession. C.O.P.S. has served more than thirty thousand separate families since 1984. Members include spouses, children, parents, siblings, significant others, and affected co-workers of officers killed in the line of duty

C.O.P.S. provides counseling services, scholarship money, and other vital resources to help these distraught families rebuild their shattered lives.

At about the same time that Eileen Vitale was volunteering at the charity golf event, the Saugus town manager approached the Vitale family, wanting to honor their fallen officer. Harold was only the second policeman ever killed in town, which was incorporated more than two centuries ago.

A tract of land near the Saugus River was dedicated as the Officer Harold L. Vitale Memorial Park. The family decided to start a foundation in their brother's name, and fund it with the proceeds of road races that they envisioned beginning and ending in the newly christened park. "Our initial goal was to develop a reserve fund to assist with the park's upkeep, and hopefully generate additional money to fund a scholarship for a deserving high

school kid in Revere, and another in Saugus," adds Dick Vitale, also a CPA.

The initial road race was a success, not only because of Harold's popularity among friends, fellow officers and townspeople, but also due to his extended family. His mom had a dozen siblings herself, and consequently, in addition to the seven surviving Vitale kids there were upwards of fifty cousins, most of whom stuck around greater Boston.

"That inaugural race and the dedication of the park was the first time since Harold died that we as a family collectively felt a sense of pride, of peace, of honor," states Les Vitale. "Until then we had only felt shock, horror and outrage, not just at his untimely death, but also because of the remorselessness of his

killer, the lenience of the sentence; the whole ordeal was like a nightmare that lasted for years."

Despite the size of the nuclear and extended family, Les Vitale uses an odd word to describe his feelings: loneliness. "I always felt it was hard for others to understand what we went through, but with the park's dedication and the robust turnout for the race, we started to feel that Harold hadn't died in vain."

When Eileen suggested a golf tournament to supplement the road race, it wasn't a hard sell, as several of the Vitale brothers were avid golfers. "We hoped to break even at worst, and raise awareness regarding the dangers of police work," explains Dick. "We wanted to reinforce to our attendees that it's a job that requires a weapon, and regular dealings with criminals, criminal behavior and society's underbelly."

That first golf event in 1994 was modestly profitable, so the family decided to consult with some business associates and family friends who could help them make a greater impact with the event. Over the subsequent decades, the added experience and expertise through their networks has allowed them to raise more than a million dollars. The tournament now nets six figures annually, and funds more scholarships than they ever thought possible.

There is always a police presence at the annual golf event. Dana Bates was sworn in as an officer back in 1972, the same year as Harold Vitale, and has never missed the tournament. George Hart was the officer in charge the night Harold was killed, and broke the tragic news to Eileen and the family. He has also been a regular presence at the tournament over the years.

The Officer Harold L. Vitale Memorial Fund provides grants to C.O.P.S. and the National Law Enforcement Memorial Fund, and provides the aforementioned scholarships. Many of the high school scholarships end up in the hands of the children of current, retired or fallen officers. "Not only do they inherently understand the importance of the police in our lives, they also have the financial need, owing to the poorly paid nature of the profession," states Les Vitale. "It's also gratifying to know these scholarship applicants are learning about Harold, his story, his history in the area. They are saying his name, thirty years after he's gone. There's true satisfaction in that."

According to C.O.P.S., about 150 police officers are killed on the job annually, which means more than 4,500 have made the ultimate sacrifice since Harold Vitale died during the Reagan Administration. All are mourned by their loved ones, as is Harold by his immediate and extended family. "He is sorely missed every day," concludes Les Vitale. "It's an understatement to say they don't make them like Harold anymore."

For more information
visit: www.vitalememorialfund.org

Walking with Anthony
Charity Celebrity Golf Tournament

Life can change on a dime. Nobody knows that harsh reality better than the victim of a spinal cord injury.

"It was the best weekend of my life. Then it was instantly the worst weekend of my life." So begins Anthony Purcell, who was living large at the 2010 Super Bowl in Miami, reveling in the excitement and festivities, and loving life with his cousins, including an NFL player who was helping provide behind-the-scenes access around town. Anthony was at the beach and took off with a running start towards the waves, displaying the same exuberance of any athletic, high-spirited 22-year old. He belly-flopped into the waves, hit an unseen sandbar, and broke his neck, severely injuring his C-5 and C-6 vertebrae. In an instant, his life, and the lives of his parents, brothers and sister, changed forever.

Fortunately, he was taken to the renowned Jackson Memorial Hospital and operated on by prominent spinal surgeon Allan Levi. Unfortunately, the hospital's protocol was to release him just twenty one days later, strapped to an electric wheelchair with virtually zero mobility. Insurance would cover no more of this horrific injury.

The Purcells were shocked to learn of Anthony's imminent discharge. "Kicked to the curb," explains his mother, disgustedly. Micki Purcell is a Type A business titan with numerous concerns and in the instant it took for Anthony to break his neck, she and Anthony's father Joe rerouted their intense focus. Getting their son off a gurney, restoring his independence and getting him back to a semblance of a normal life were set as the goals, and they marshaled their considerable resources and force of will to make it happen.

"He couldn't eat, nor sit up, nor fend for himself in any way. We immediately paid exorbitantly out-of-pocket to extend his stay." The additional time

in rehab proved just marginally helpful, and Anthony's parents discovered that "compensation" was the watchword at a typical rehab hospital and that spinal cord injury (SCI) patients were trained to live within the serious constraints of their new reality. Undaunted, they searched out more aggressive treatment for their son, first going to California and a rehab center called Project Walk, then eventually finding a dynamo of a strength trainer in Michigan named Mike Barwis, who has helped Anthony fight and claw unrelentingly for every incremental gain.

"My son can drive, he can bench press nearly two hundred pounds, he has progressed to leg braces. He not only holds an important sales job, but he's one of the top salespeople in a large company. He has a girlfriend," continues his smiling mother, with understandable pride. "Our son has gotten his life back. Our goal at Walking With Anthony is to help others with SCI improve in a similar fashion, get off the couch, out of bed, to stop languishing and get back into the world. The most important thing we can give someone is hope. Our mission is to provide both emotional and financial support to those dealing with an SCI, the accident victim and their loved ones."

The stark reality is that aggressively and comprehensively treating an SCI results in a six-figure tab annually. The vast majority of sufferers cannot begin to foot the bill, and the fallout is severe: homes are lost, marriages dissolve, relationships founder, motivation and optimism disappear. One recipient at a time, Walking With Anthony helps get them the rehab they desperately need and essential equipment to allow measurable improvement. Unfortunately, the foundation gets thirty applications a month, and can only help a handful annually. This is where their full-volume golf event comes in, which debuted in 2013 and has taken off like an express train since.

"The golf event is a major part of our fundraising," explains Micki, "and we treat it with the same seriousness of purpose as a business. We laid the groundwork, the infrastructure, put our reputation for integrity on the line, and realized if we pulled out all stops, the monetary benefit to our foundation would come back exponentially."

According to the founder, the inaugural event required some begging and even a few giveaways to fill the field. One year later, it sold out in two weeks. "We went from a handful of Redskin players on hand to twenty," states Micki, a D.C.-area native with ten siblings, nearly thirty nieces and nephews, and an octogenarian mother, a former judge, among her support system in and around the capital.

In the same way an SCI rehab is an expensive proposition, so too is this unique golf event. What it lacks in longevity it makes up for with impact. The tournament, conducted at the prestigious Country Club of Fairfax in Virginia, is peppered with rec-

ognizable politicians, significant government officials, influential businesspeople, athletes and various other VIP types, all used to high-end treatment. "More than a few have told us, 'I will make sure to never miss this tournament.' The food, the gifts, the niceties, festivities, the special touches on every hole, they add up to an unforgettable event, and our participants rave about the experience," states Micki, who divides her time between Florida and Southern California. "We are completely volunteer-based, no salaries whatsoever, and every penny we take in goes back to help SCI victims get the rehab and equipment they need to get their lives back."

"There are 13,000 significant spinal cord injuries occurring in the U.S. every year, thirty-five per day on average, and each one happens out of the blue, in a heartbeat." So concludes Micki Purcell, who wishes she had the financial resources to assist all victims, and

not the small fraction she currently can. "But unlike cancer or diabetes sufferers, most people don't personally know anyone confined to a wheelchair due to an SCI. Our fundraising efforts are mostly successful, but we also get turned down. I'll thank them for their time regardless, while thinking, I hope they never slip on a banana peel. It can happen in a split of a second."

For more information visit: www.walkingwithanthony.org

Women Golfers Give Back Annual Tournament

Despite a concerted effort by the golf industry to be more inclusive of women, children, and minorities, in the eyes of many the game remains part of the old boys network. Regardless of the inherent difficulty of getting that tiny ball into that elusive hole with efficiency, another barrier to entry is the intimidation factor. Ladies Day, red tees and the women's locker room are part of the vernacular, but golf hasn't always been overly welcoming towards women. Philadelphian A.K. Frazier and the organization she founded known as Women Golfers Give Back are trying to change that perception, one girl at a time.

If one were to make a blueprint for the ideal individual to initiate a charity effort like this one, it would look a lot like A.K. Frazier. First, she is an accomplished player who once reached the finals of the U.S. Women's Senior Amateur. But more importantly, she has a long history in the world of non-profit organizations. She serves as the executive director of the Valentine Foundation, which funds social change for women and girls in greater Philadelphia.

"My professional life and private life are totally different, and I wanted to find a way to somehow merge them," begins the mother of three. "The Valentine Foundation serves those from lower socioeconomic backgrounds. Among other things, we attempt to make women leaders more effective and foster the next generation. But away from the office I play competitive golf at a nice private club, and have met, competed against and befriended literally hundreds of people all over the map. I wanted to find a way to put both halves together into a whole."

The idea for the charity germinated at a conference where a speaker discussed how groups of people with a common interest could pool their money for philanthropic purposes. "That was very appealing to me, as I realized I knew so many women golfers who might be

interested and who understood the need for girls to be exposed to golf."

The speaker emphasized that the gifts of time, effort and creativity were just as crucial as money, so Frazier recruited a small cadre of her peers, women well versed in the game, and they got to work collectively. WGGB was formed in 2003. Over the years, many dozens of dedicated committee members and volunteers have helped grow the program far beyond what the founders of this unique organization ever thought possible.

"The game has given me so much," continues the former Pennsylvania State Women's Senior Amateur champion. "Socially, competitively, and has allowed me to meet people and travel to places I never would have imagined. I thought it would be great to expose young women who otherwise wouldn't have the opportunity to learn the game, and perhaps use it to someday better their own lives."

WGGB began by making grants to existing programs like The First Tee and LPGA/USGA Girls Golf. But these are feeder programs, and the girls were aging out of them just as competitive opportunities presented

themselves. So the organization developed something called the Players' Program, geared towards teens. Now funding a half-dozen separate programs around Philadelphia, each with eight to fifteen attendees and their own golf instructor, the idea is to keep the girls competitively focused. Most either join the high school girls team or find a spot on the boys team, but some have even taken the initiative to start a girls team at their local high school if one does not exist.

"We've had girls get full scholarships to schools like Purdue, Notre Dame, Kansas and Rollins College. We even have several alumni on the LPGA Tour," relates Frazier. More important than these few making the big leagues is the fact that all the girls who stay the course gain confidence, maturity, and develop the unique skill to play the game with enough competence to help insure a brighter future. "Women have been missing out on all the business opportunities that take place on the golf course. Our program empowers young women, gives them the tools they need to use golf as a springboard to greater success in life."

WGGB's annual golf tournament is the engine that funds the entire organization. Virtually every dollar the organization collects to fund its programs comes courtesy of their annual event, held at the prestigious Sunnybrook Golf Club in Philadelphia. "We are all volunteers," offers the founder. "We generally raise about eighty thousand dollars the day of the tournament, and that is our operating budget for the following year." She gives full credit to the Bryn Mawr Trust Company, the event's lead sponsor. "Without their support we would have great difficulty in raising meaningful money. We are delighted that they support this cause so enthusiastically."

"Furthermore, Sunnybrook is very generous in that they invite up to sixty of our students out for the morning, before the event itself. They let our more advanced students actually play the course," explains Frazier. "The younger girls benefit from a clinic put on by teaching professionals. We feed them all lunch, and then our generous donors take to the course in the afternoon."

Their annual golf event is followed by a dinner and live auction, usually emceed by long-time Philadelphia TV sports personality Dei Lynam.

"I don't do many events like these," begins Lynam, the daughter of former NBA head coach Jim Lynam. "But WGGB is such a great organization. I only wish they had been around when I was a kid; I would hopefully be a much better player. I took up golf in my late twenties, and even though I love the game it can be incredibly challenging!"

A.K. Frazier continues to play competitively and promote WGGB, despite the challenges inherent in each endeavor. "Golf has given me so much, it changed my life. It is WGGB's mission to use the game as a tool to change and better the lives of girls in our area, and help them achieve more than they might have otherwise."

For more information visit: www.womengolfersgiveback.org

The World's Largest Golf Outing (WLGO)

WORLD'S LARGEST GOLF OUTING™

A BILLY CASPER GOLF EVENT

There are some jumbo-sized golf galas chronicled within these pages. Five hundred golfers gathering in Chicago, four hundred in Mississippi, three hundred each in Georgia and Michigan, to name but a few.

However, all of these charity jamborees, and dozens of others that are nearly as colossal, are like a candlelit dinner for two compared to the WLGO.

The numbers relating to the 2014 iteration tell the story in dramatic fashion. More than twelve thousand golfers participating on nearly 120 golf courses in twenty-seven states. Almost fifty thousand golf balls were used and more than eight hundred thousand total strokes were taken. Most importantly, nearly $900,000 was raised for the Wounded Warrior Project.

The World's Largest Golf Outing is the brainchild of Billy Casper Golf chairman and CEO Peter Hill. The event is driven by the company's six thousand peak-season employees, their business partners, and most of all by loyal golfers. The Wounded Warrior Project is an ideal cause to support, because before commencing his hall-of-fame golf career, company namesake Billy Casper served in the Navy himself. Years later, after he became one of the PGA Tour's most established stars, he entertained U.S. troops in Asia by hitting golf balls off aircraft carriers.

Despite his many on-course achievements, Casper was overshadowed through much of his career by "The Big Three" of Arnold Palmer, Jack Nicklaus and Gary Player. Though marketing power and name recognition didn't easily come his way, the wins certainly did. More than fifty on the PGA Tour, including three major championships. The ultimate irony: even when he passed away early in 2015, the majority of the sports

headlines went to iconic North Carolina basketball coach Dean Smith, who died the same week.

Because Casper's profile was always somewhat lower than his peers, it would surprise most avid golfers to learn that Billy Casper Golf is the largest owner-operator of golf courses, country clubs, and resorts in the United States, with more than 150 properties in nearly thirty states. The company directs all aspects of club operations, golf and grounds maintenance, staffing and training, clubhouse operations, food and beverage, merchandising, golf instruction, marketing and public relations, special events and financial management.

"Some years ago, Peter Hill wanted to find a novel way for the company to give back to the community. Hence, World's Largest Golf Outing was born," explains

Rich Katz, a senior vice-president at Billy Casper Golf. "The event has become an incredibly powerful tool to raise awareness and funds for injured servicemen and women who risk their lives to protect ours. A side benefit is that a charity fundraising event of this magnitude inspires people to either begin playing, or continue playing the great game of golf, which has seen a decline in participation in the last decade or more."

Part of golf's problem in retaining players and attracting newcomers is the inherent expense of the game. Look no further than the dozens of chapters preceding this one. Many charity golf events, including numerous examples showcased in this book, are far from inexpensive. It's part and parcel for raising meaningful monies for the charity in

question. The WLGO, by contrast, is an everyman event. Green fees to participate at any BCG-operated facility range from thirty dollars up to little more than a hundred, with ten dollars of every golfer's entry fee benefitting the Wounded Warrior Project. Even better, all additional donations given by players and non-players are earmarked for the same cause.

"We are deeply moved by the outpouring of support from golfers and veterans alike," says Adam Silva, Chief Development Officer of Wounded Warrior Project. "We salute Billy Casper Golf for its altruistic culture and presenting this massive event with tremendous precision and professionalism."

The beauty of the one-day event is that it goes far beyond a day of golf and a huge check to this worthy cause. Nearly four hundred injured soldiers participated in the 2014 WLGO, allowing thousands of supporters to meet them and hear their stories. "Our fundraising efforts have exceeded what we thought possible," continues Katz. "But it's not just fundraising that counts. It's the wounded warriors themselves who latch onto golf to help cope with and overcome challenges. Playing side by side with wounded warriors during the WLGO is emotional and rewarding for our participants. They are truly heroes."

Even though the event takes place more than a month after the Fourth of July, it is just as patriotic. Many courses honor the military with moments of silence, ceremonial tee shots, standing ovations, national anthems and color guards before play. There are patriotic decorations course-wide, golf carts adorned in red, white and blue, military vehicles, and flyovers on-site. Brass bands, local politicians and high school marching bands lend the whole event an air of Americana that is rarely seen in society anymore.

"Our nation's generosity and the growth of the World's Largest Golf Outing is amazing," says WLGO founder Hill. "It's humbling to witness the unwavering appreciation for our brave troops whose sacrifices protect and preserve our daily freedoms. It is intensely gratifying to know we have helped raise in excess of two million dollars since the event's inception just a few short years ago."

Equally gratifying is to know that so many thousands of appreciative citizens give their time, effort, and hard-earned money to support our unsung heroes in the military.

For more information visit: www.worldslargestgolfouting.com

The Young Life Buffalo South Charity Tournament

At most charity golf tournaments the highlight of the day is just that-the tournament itself. But in western New York at the Young Life Buffalo South event, three decades have proved otherwise. The day's highlight comes via personal testimony at the evening banquet. Year after year, the room becomes hushed as a teenager or two steps to the podium, often in a tentative fashion and with a quavering voice, to share with hundreds of adult strangers the positive transformation that Jesus has made in their lives.

It's the heartfelt five-minute speeches that leave the room riveted. Kids talk about how they were headed down the wrong roads in life, dealing with both internal and external turmoil, and how the Young Life organization helped change their courses. Don Meyer, an area lumber executive who co-founded the tournament in 1985, tells of meeting a tournament golfer in a social setting. "He told me he played in our event a decade prior and had no recollection of the round, the meal or the prizes won. But he said he would never forget the poignancy of what he heard from those young people at dinner."

Though Meyer's affiliation with the tournament stretches back more than thirty years, that's only half as long as he's been associated with Young Life. Raised in a conservative Christian home in his native Chicago, he became a Young Life leader to teenagers while in college. He relished the opportunity to give back to the group after finding business success, and estimates that the golf tournament he co-founded has raised more than two million dollars for Young Life since that inaugural event during the Reagan administration netted an exceedingly modest $2,500.

Nathan Stoddard is the area director for Young Life Buffalo South and has been on the job for over a dozen years. "The organization's goal is twofold and hasn't really changed since it was founded in 1940. We strive to introduce Jesus Christ into the lives of young people and let Jesus be their guide and leader."

The organization uses volunteer leaders, who fan out to schools, local gyms, sporting events and other locations where teens gather. Sometimes teens who are already involved with the group are the initial point of contact. They attempt to engage kids in conversation, get to know them, and invite them to a Young Life meeting, which is typically held in the home of a teen member. The meetings feature contemporary music, games, improvised skits, and end with a faith-based song and a short story on the life of Jesus.

"Some kids are one and done," explains Stoddard. "Others learn to love the group dynamic and decide to come regularly and even end up as leaders themselves. But no matter how much they like or don't like a meeting, we never ostracize those who forgo our organization, nor do we pressure anyone to take part."

Stoddard's goal is to make a weekly, one-hour Young Life meeting the highlight of a kid's week, and there's an established precedent to that mindset. The organization has expanded dramatically through the decades and has branches in all fifty states and forty-five countries internationally.

"Kids always have problems, whether overt or covert. Even the so-called straight arrows, the athletes and leaders, can be lonely, disillusioned or suffer low self-esteem. Other kids might be partying too much, into drugs, maybe promiscuous. Others have family issues, a broken home, an abusive or alcoholic parent. Some kids internalize their turmoil by self-mutilation or cutting themselves, which is a more recent phenomenon," relates Stoddard.

Meyer, who has been in Buffalo for some sixty years, adds, "Our primary focus is to make kids feel comfortable at meetings, and the formula is time-tested. There is no doubt when kids get involved and invite Jesus into their lives, problems start to resolve. When they feel confident in their relationship with Jesus, then the peer pressure, harsh judgment and other pitfalls

of adolescence start to diminish."

The highlight for many kids is going to one of twenty-seven Young Life camps during the summer. At these camps the days are filled with adventure activities — parasailing, high rope courses, tubing, sailing, mountain climbing, beach volleyball, basketball, and more. Some kids are so changed from one week at a Young Life camp that they become volunteers on a work crew for a month the next summer. These volunteers cook, clean, do maintenance and help out wherever possible. "Many young people feel so strongly about the experiences they have enjoyed as campers themselves, they feel the need to give back and let others experience the same joy," says Stoddard.

Stoddard concludes, "We're grateful for the Young Life golf tournament that provides more than half of the revenue needed to operate Young Life in Buffalo South. And we're pleased and thankful for all the loyal corporate and individual sponsors who make this tournament possible."

**For more information visit:
www.buffalosouth.younglife.org**